In *Resolve*, Will Ertel has provided young people with an eminently practical guide to the management of finances that is grounded in biblical principles of stewardship and peppered with appreciable wit. Will's style is straightforward and accessible, making sound approaches to the handling of personal finances easily understandable to the lay reader. This is a book I want my own children and all the students I serve to read.

Dr. J. Derek Halvorson
President, Covenant College, Lookout Mountain, GA

Many are intimidated by money matters and believe that money experts speak a foreign language. Will makes important concepts understandable through clear explanations, practical examples, and helpful illustrations. While this book would benefit people of all ages, I expect that it will become my go-to book for pre-marriage counseling and helping young adults to mature in their understanding of financial wisdom.

Dr. James Newheiser, Jr.
Director of Christian Counseling, Reformed Theological Seminary, Charlotte, NC and author of *Money, Debt, and Finances*

My wife and I have raised three children, now all married and, in their thirties, and I have spent the past 13 years working with students at Liberty University. This book is everything I want my children and students to know and do when it comes to their personal finances. *Resolve* approaches this subject with a Biblical Worldview and is perfect for the individual or couple who desire to integrate their faith into the decisions they make about finances. Will does a perfect job of walking a young person(s) through the various financial decisions that need to be made while in school and certainly during the first ten years after graduation. His personal stories and examples are great fun. I know from personal experience that the decisions we make in our twenties will impact us in a significant way for the rest of our lives. This should be required reading for every Christian young person from age 18 to 30.

Kurt Cornfield
Financial Planning Professor, Liberty University, Lynchburg, VA

Will writes with brevity, clarity and conviction on matters that twentysomethings need to be thinking about, especially with regard to how to view money matters through a biblical worldview, and how to implement specific strategies that resolve to honor God with our finances. Anyone will benefit from the godly principles in this book, but especially those in their twenties.

Sarah Ivill
Mother, Author, Bible Teacher, Retreat and Conference Speaker

This helpful book on financial planning is built on the foundations of biblical stewardship, emphasizing key biblical imperatives such as generosity, tithing, contentment and living in light of eternity. Will Ertel has given us a helpful guide to wise stewardship of what God has given to us, including both principles and practical ways to invest. It is well-written, accessible (even for the non-financially astute—like me!), and full of helpful illustrations. I plan to give a copy to my children and recommend it to the young adults in my church.

Dr. William B. Barcley
Senior Pastor, Sovereign Grace Presbyterian Church (PCA), Charlotte, NC

Will's financial expertise and pastoral heart were united all throughout the work. He gives biblical, understandable, and applicable advice on wise resource stewardship—I was happy to have many of our own family practices confirmed as well as adjusted by Will's advice. As a good friend to those who want to do better management, Will's exhortations don't judge or demean but gently instruct on when and how to save, spend, and invest. I would highly recommend this book for parents to review and to share with their adult children.

Dr. Gabe Sylvia
Senior Pastor, Christ Our Hope Church (PCA), Wake Forest, NC

Stewardship is something of inestimable value entrusted by the King for kingdom purposes. *Resolve* is the embodiment of this kind of sound stewardship. Will Ertel's financial wisdom entrusted to his readers is a valuable tool.

Karen Hodge
Coordinator of Women's Ministries for the Presbyterian Church in America (PCA) and author of *Transformed: Life-taker to Life-giver* and *Life-giving Leadership*

As a father, marriage and couples coach, and former pastor - I am thrilled to recommend the rich resource of *Resolve.* Will's intentionality to address with wisdom, experience, and excellence the topic of financial stewardship is a breath of fresh air to a generation that needs to rekindle the embers of financial understanding. I am excited to see this topic and this book address the self-sacrifice, discipline, and hard work God requires for us to truly live a life of freedom, purpose, and intentionality. I know many will benefit from this resource - I can't wait to see this tool encourage, inspire, and challenge the next generation to be intentional in the important arena of finances. The design of generosity and financial integrity is a hallmark of our love, a characteristic our world is eager to see lived with the purpose to inspire and impact a watching world.

Ken Norwood
Leadership Coach at Kenergy Coaching

RESOLVE

RESOLVE

A Personal Financial Planning Book for Twentysomethings Getting Serious About Stewardship

Will Ertel

Matthews, North Carolina

Resolve
A Personal Financial Planning Book for Twentysomethings
Getting Serious About Stewardship

Edited by Rebecca C. Kicklighter

Contact *oikonomiapress@gmail.com* for inquiries on paperback orders of 25 or more books.

ISBN 979-8-98774-620-2 (paperback)
ISBN 979-8-98774-621-9 (eBook)

RESOLVE

RESOLVE

A Personal Financial Planning Book for Twentysomethings Getting Serious About Stewardship

Will Ertel

Matthews, North Carolina

Resolve
A Personal Financial Planning Book for Twentysomethings
Getting Serious About Stewardship

Edited by Rebecca C. Kicklighter

Contact *oikonomiapress@gmail.com* for inquiries on paperback orders of 25 or more books.

This book is for informational and educational purposes only. Nothing in this book is to be considered investment advice, tax advice, or financial advice. Do not make any financial planning or investment decisions without first talking to an investment advisor. Past performance does not predict future results. Tassel Capital Management is a registered investment advisor with the U.S. Securities and Exchange Commission.

ISBN 979-8-98774-620-2 (paperback)
ISBN 979-8-98774-621-9 (eBook)

DEDICATION

This book is dedicated to my wife, life partner, and best friend, Debbie. Our journey through marriage, parenthood, and life has been our great adventure together. Debbie has always been an encouraging partner in our stewardship responsibilities and in our desire to teach and model what we believe and know to be true.

DEDICATION

This book is dedicated to my wife, life partner, and best friend, Debbie. Our journey through marriage, parenthood, and life has been our great adventure together. Debbie has always been an encouraging partner in our stewardship responsibilities and in our desire to teach and model what we believe and know to be true.

TABLE OF CONTENTS

PREFACE

Hannah, Leah, and Elizabeth,

This book is not perfect. Perfect, as it is often said, is the enemy of excellent. In the same way, excellent can be the enemy of pretty good, and pretty good can be the enemy of completed. I have decided to not let the pursuit of excellence be the reason why this book was never completed.

All books are communication tools that allow one person to communicate something to a large number of people; this makes books inherently impersonal. You need to read this book and carefully consider the *personal* implications of each principle as you approach your financial decision-making. In this sense, *Resolve* is intensely personal. I am not trying to give you a financial reference book or a long to-do list. I am sharing five exhortations and providing observations that I believe will help you pursue successful stewardship as an adult.

- Give charitably.
- Set and take action on financial goals.
- Create margin.
- Save and invest your margin.
- Plan your estate.

According to dictionary.com, an exhortation is "an address or communication emphatically urging someone to do something." I urge you to embrace and implement these five exhortations and they will provide an excellent foundation for you as a steward of your resources.

I believe the Bible is true, and I have raised you to live according to the Truth. Not surprisingly, you will find a number of references to specific Bible verses and passages in this book. While the Bible contains stewardship principles that are transcendent, their origin in the Bible (whether it be in specific passages or pervasive themes) may not make them convincing, or even persuasive, to others. That's fine. Understanding the principles, applying them, and enjoying the good outcomes that result are not contingent on believing in the ultimate source. You don't have to be a physicist, after all, to know that gravity exists and that dropping your phone will result in it smashing to the ground.

While my categorization of cash outflow into Convictions, Requirements, and Lifestyle Spending is unique, the five exhortations elaborated on in this book are ultimately not new or groundbreaking. Writers like Ron Blue, Larry Burkett, Howard Dayton, Russ Crosson, Randy Alcorn, and others have provided sound instruction on how to apply Biblical truth to personal finance. I have been greatly blessed and influenced by their insight.

The Certified Kingdom Advisor® professional organization teaches that five money management principles[1] are Biblical, and, therefore, transcendent. These Biblical principles have clearly influenced my thinking and convictions.

You will likely think of Leah's famous line, "I should have made a sign," when you read about the long walk at the end of chapter 3. I do hope the content, along with the packaging and presentation, will capture your heart and mind the way it has mine.

The decade of your twenties is bookended by complete financial dependence on one end and, humanly speaking, financial independence on the other. Choices you make in this ten-year time span will begin to solidify life-defining financial habits. Done

---

[1] Certified Kingdom Advisor material lists five transcendent money management principles: give generously, avoid the use of debt, set long-term goals, spend less than you earn, and build liquidity and margin.

well, these habits can help build a reliable framework for success as a steward that will bless you for your entire lifetime.

My prayer is that you will not waste the opportunities in front of you in your twenties. Understanding and agreeing that these are good ideas is not enough. I have seen many who wholeheartedly agree that these five exhortations are good and worthwhile but who have failed to implement them.

In Daniel 1:8, Daniel "resolved that he would not defile himself" by eating the king's food even though the decision would bring about great personal harm. While poor stewardship habits will not bring on imminent death, as it likely would have for Daniel, you must develop the resolve to implement these principles *because they are hard to do*. You will not do them naturally. Many of your peers, even those serious about stewardship, will not practice them.

I pray that the material presented here reinforces what you are doing well and also serves as a catalyst to prompt you to think rightly about money and financial decision-making. May we strive together to one day hear the words from the gospel of Matthew Chapter 21, verse 23: "Well done, good and faithful servant. Enter into the joy of your master."

I love you,

Daddy

February 2023

INTRODUCTION

I had quite the reputation among the bank tellers who worked across the street from my office. Nothing made them look busier than me entering the lobby; all heads went down, and everyone began counting something: paper clips, blank deposit slips, anything to look busy.

At the end of each month, I would walk in with my printed spreadsheets and approach a teller. I always asked to make three different withdrawals – one for each daughter. Each withdrawal request had a specific coin and bill breakdown.

The specifics of the $79 withdrawal for the monthly allowance, were designed to allow a twelve-year-old to easily make the change necessary to give $7.90 to the church, give me $7.90 to add to her investment account, and then have small enough denominations left over to allow her to be comfortable carrying the money around.

Tens	2
Fives	7
Ones	22
Quarters	6
Dimes	4
Nickels	2
	$ 79

Once the teller processed the first withdrawal, I produced the second request and then my third. I left with three envelopes full of bills and coins every month. I'm pretty confident those transactions were not helping the bank make any money. I'm very confident that the teller would recognize me the next month and appear too busy to repeat the tedious task.

That evening I had three conversations, each on a different bed, with a different daughter, spreadsheet, and envelope. The conversation was usually brief and covered the spreadsheet listing the spending categories that were now their personal responsibility. They took custody of the envelope and its valuable, jangling, and seemingly life-giving contents.

The monthly work to define budget categories, the calculus problems to figure out the optimal combination of coins and bills, and the monthly bank withdrawals did not happen without time and effort on my part. It took work, but the goal was to give each daughter ownership of some money and some choices. Saving for a camera or an upcoming concert was the longest horizon they seemed to be able to imagine – but they participated.

Each daughter is now launched financially (at least mostly) and in every other way, as well. Unfortunately, the lessons from the envelopes and spreadsheets may not be enough for them now. Hopefully, the lessons to give, save and think carefully about where they most wanted to spend money formed a good foundation. These principles still work, of course, but navigating financial decision-making as independent adults between the ages of twenty and thirty is much more complex.

The decade of their twenties provides so many opportunities that they can't afford to waste. These five exhortations must be turned into habits. There must be the resolve to implement these five principles, but ultimately trust cannot be placed in the effort.

> *Trust in the Lord with all your heart, and do not lean on your own understanding. In all your ways acknowledge him, and he will make straight your paths.* **Proverbs 3:5-6**

Exhortation One

GIVE CHARITABLY

Early in 2002, after 600 years of use, France officially stopped using the French franc as legal tender. As part of a continent-wide adoption of a new currency called the Euro, the French allowed all francs to be converted to Euros at a rate of 6.55957 Francs to 1 Euro.

It was announced that after February 17, 2002, the French francs would not be accepted as payment for goods or services in France. By law, the National Bank of France would exchange French franc bills (but not coins) for Euros for a ten-year period, and then, after February 17, 2012, no French franc bills could be exchanged at any bank. They would no longer have a monetary value.

△ △ △ △ △ △

It may seem counterproductive to suggest that in order to meet financial goals and ambitions your first commitment should be to build a habit of giving money away. "Give charitably" suggests you take hard-earned money and, instead of spending it to provide for yourself and your family, saving it for a rainy day, or investing it for an important future goal, you give it away. Instead of a step backward, cultivating a habit of giving is the first, and most important, step toward progress as a steward. Giving fosters significant and meaningful progress toward learning to be content with the financial resources God provides through your vocation and circumstances.

The exhortation to give charitably is based on clear Biblical teaching, my personal experiences, and direct observations of hundreds of clients who have made a lifetime habit of giving regularly, giving generously, and giving sacrificially.

What the Bible Says about Giving

The Bible teaches that God's followers should give. Biblical encouragements to give span the entire Bible from the Old Testament thru the New Testament:

> *The best of the firstfruits of your ground you shall bring into the house of the Lord your God.* **Exodus 23:19**

> *Bring the full tithe into the storehouse.* **Malachi 3:10a**

> *As for the rich in this present age, charge them . . . to do good, to be rich in good works, to be generous and ready to share.* **I Timothy 6:17–18**

Some who affirm the Bible as authoritative but are reluctant to give a tithe often cite the absence of New Testament teachings on the tithe. This is not convincing for two reasons.

First, Jesus acknowledges that the Pharisees were rightly tithing on all their crops (even their spices) when he said, "These you ought to have done" in Matthew 23:23. The rebuke to the Pharisees that followed was because of their neglect of the underlying purpose of the law—justice, mercy, and faithfulness. Jesus was not condemning their practice of tithing.

Secondly, the ceremonial laws and the sacrificial systems of the Old Testament did find their fulfillment in the person of

Christ. As followers of Christ, we are now set free from these rituals. The New Testament clearly teaches, however, that the duties and obligations of obedience are not less stringent than under the Old Testament laws, but rather they are more stringent. In the Sermon on the Mount throughout Matthew Chapter 5, Jesus repeatedly says, "You have heard it said . . ."[2] and continues to explain how more is required to conform our hearts to the law than just our outward actions.

Since the New Testament does not assert that less sacrifice is required of New Testament Christians, we should not assume that we can give less than a tithe and be faithful and obedient. I do not think that Americans in 2023 are asked to give less than impoverished followers of Christ were asked to give in the first century.

The Bible Has Instructions for How to Give

As I have grown in my understanding and appreciation for the Biblical teaching on giving, I see more and more compelling passages that instruct God's followers on *how to* give.

Giving should be done as a first priority.

> *Honor the LORD with your wealth and with the firstfruits of all your produce . . .* **Proverbs 3:9**

Giving should be done with joy.

> *Each one must give as he has decided in his heart, not reluctantly or under compulsion, for God loves a cheerful giver.* **II Corinthians 9:7**

---

[2] In Matthew Chapter 5, Jesus makes this remark in verse 21 regarding anger, verse 27 regarding lust, verse 33 regarding oaths, verse 38 regarding retaliation, and in verse 42 regarding love.

Giving should be done regularly.

> *On the first day of every week, each of you is to put something aside and store it up, as he may prosper so that there will be no collecting when I come.* **I Corinthians 16:2**

Giving should be sacrificial.

> *Jesus looked up and saw the rich putting their gifts into the offering box, and he saw a poor widow put in two small copper coins. And he said, "Truly, I tell you, this poor widow has put in more than all of them. For they all contributed out of their abundance, but she out of her poverty put in all she had to live on."* **Luke 21:1–4**
>
> *But the king said to Araunah, 'No, but I will buy it from you for a price. I will not offer burnt offerings to the LORD my God that cost me nothing.'* **II Samuel 24:24**

Proper Motivation for Giving

The Bible teaches that *a proper motivation for giving* is an essential part of your full participation in the spiritual blessings that come from your giving. First Corinthians 13 is a very common chapter about love. Look at what it says in the first three verses ***(emphasis added)***:

> *If I speak in the tongues of men and of angels, but have not love, I am a noisy gong or a clanging cymbal. And if I have prophetic powers, and understand all mysteries and all knowledge, and if I have all faith, so as to remove mountains, but have not love, I am nothing.* ***If I give away all I have,*** *and if I deliver up my body to be burned,* ***but have not love, I gain nothing. I Corinthians 13:1-3***

While giving regularly and sacrificially can provide blessings to you, beware of giving solely out of rote obedience. The passage above indicates that a motivation of love is essential.

My Experiences with Charitable Giving

From age 20 to 29, I experienced college life, my first 'real' job, marriage, my first home purchase, two job changes, and the birth of two children. Not counting a three-month minor league baseball career, I have worked my entire career in a professional capacity as an accountant or financial planner. This track has provided me with comfortable office jobs with higher-than-average pay.

From the very start of my career, my faith convictions have played a large role in my decisions to give charitably. Ever since becoming a born-again Christian in college, I have been committed to giving a minimum of ten percent of my gross income to my church.[3] While the concept of a 'Biblical tithe' was not often emphasized at churches I attended, I developed a conviction that giving ten percent of my gross income to the church I attended was both a matter of obedience and an appropriate expression of my faith.

My desire and conviction to tithe have never been driven by appeals or requests from personnel in the churches I attended. In fact, I tend to become more reluctant to give the more a person or organization prods me to do so. Instead, my passion for giving is rooted in my belief that there is truth in scripture about the non-financial benefits of giving generously.

---

[3] In this case, 'my church' means the church I attend on a weekly basis. Some have said to me, "I agree with the sentiment, but I don't feel comfortable giving that much to the church I attend." I respond, either out loud or in my head, "If you agree but don't give 10%, then you are either lying or you should seek out a different church."

My Observations of Generous Givers

I see conclusive (albeit anecdotal) evidence in the lives of others that the practice of generous giving provides many blessings that extend beyond intangible spiritual ones.

In this context, I am defining a generous giver as one who makes a habit of giving at least 10% of their gross income. These aren't super wealthy people who make $1,000,000 a year. I am talking about middle-class and affluent people who have a gross income of $40,000 to $250,000 annually and have cultivated a discipline and habit of giving away 10% or more of their income.

My experience shows that generous givers tend to have more financial freedom and financial contentment as well as a more appropriate long-term view of money.

Generous givers experience more financial freedom over time. The generous givers I know are better at limiting spending and consumption. Because of the lower level of consumption, they tend to have less anxiety as it relates to their investments. In short, generous givers are happier and experience greater financial freedom than most other people.[4]

Generous givers tend to be both happier and more content (even with less money) than those who don't give as much. I am not a psychologist, but I know there is a difference between happiness and contentment. Happiness is an emotion largely dependent on circumstances and, as a result, can come and go fairly easily. Contentment is better described as a learned satisfaction with life that is not directly tied to the circumstances of the moment. Contentment can be learned and can be chosen. The contentment observed among generous givers does not seem to be misplaced because, as mentioned above, they seem to be able

---

[4] I have certainly worked with people who have enjoyed these same outcomes without giving generously, but those who have a habit of generous giving achieve these outcomes at a higher rate.

to achieve long-term goals more readily than those who give less.

As counterintuitive as it may seem, regularly giving will help you reduce financial anxieties and promote contentment with whatever financial resources you have.

Biblical Promises Regarding Giving

The Bible promises rewards for generous and faithful giving when done with the right heart and motives. Revisiting some of the Bible verses provided earlier and broadening their context reveals that many Biblical passages that encourage giving are accompanied by the promise of rewards ***(emphasis added)***:

> *Honor the LORD with your wealth and with the firstfruits of all your produce;* ***then your barns will be filled with plenty, and your vats will be bursting with wine.*** **Proverbs 3:9-10**

> *Will man rob God? Yet you are robbing me. But you say, 'How have we robbed you?' In your tithes and contributions. You are cursed with a curse, for you are robbing me, the whole nation of you. Bring the full tithe into the storehouse, that there may be food in my house. And thereby put me to the test, says the LORD of hosts,* ***if I will not open the windows of heaven for you and pour down for you a blessing until there is no more need.*** **Malachi 3:8-10**

> *The point is this: whoever sows sparingly will also reap sparingly, and whoever sows bountifully will also reap bountifully. Each one must give as he has decided in his heart, not reluctantly or under compulsion, for God loves a cheerful giver. And* ***God is able to make all grace abound to you, so that having all sufficiency in all things***

> ***at all times, you may abound in every good work.* II Corinthians 9:6-8**
>
> *As for the rich in this present age, charge them not to be haughty, nor to set their hopes on the uncertainty of riches, but on God, who richly provides us with everything to enjoy. They are to do good, to be rich in good works, to be generous and ready to share,* ***thus storing up treasure for themselves as a good foundation for the future, so that they may take hold of that which is truly life*****. I Timothy 6:17-19**

We can find other verses that clearly show giving is rewarded:

> *Do not lay up for yourselves treasures on earth, where moth and rust destroy and where thieves break in and steal, but* ***lay up for yourselves treasures in heaven, where neither moth nor rust destroys and where thieves do not break in and steal.*** **Matthew 6:19-20**
>
> *Instead, seek his kingdom, and* ***these things will be added to you****. Fear not, little flock, for it is your Father's good pleasure to give you the kingdom. Sell your possessions, and give to the needy.* ***Provide yourselves with moneybags that do not grow old, with a treasure in the heavens that does not fail, where no thief approaches and no moth destroys.*** **Luke 12:31-34**

When taken in the context of the whole Bible, these rewards are not always obvious, but the Bible's teaching on the benefits of giving can serve as a motivator to be generous.

Beware of thinking that generous giving, genuine giving that provides material and meaningful blessings to others in your community, is part of a transaction. Biblical promises about the benefits of giving generously do not turn God into a debtor required to provide you with material blessings in this life. This is not a quid pro quo or a cosmic "You scratch my back, and I'll scratch yours."

To the extent you are interested in Biblical teachings on giving, I urge you to examine the Bible for yourself. You can find tremendous resources that point to hundreds of Bible passages. Commentaries can help you understand these passages in their appropriate context. The short list of great resources for you to pursue certainly includes Randy Alcorn's *Money, Possessions, and Eternity*.[5]

The Bible's teaching about giving has universal application - that is, even if you don't personally view the Bible as an inspired and authoritative resource in your life, it contains much wisdom. Ultimately, your decisions to give charitably are a matter of conviction and certainly unity, if married. I have found that practices of prayer and meditation are essential to developing united goals and desires around giving.

Don't be intimidated by others' giving. Start early while it feels proportionately smaller. Many generous givers earned much less money thirty years ago, so giving away $20,000 out of a $200,000 income now does not seem inordinately high to them. Beginning to give generously may seem overwhelming to someone who makes $120,000 and presently gives away $0. Start where you are but commit to generous giving.

More than being rich, more than accumulating stuff, and more than feeling financially independent, people desire to be content. Many believe that being wealthy or financially independent will create that contentment; it won't. Imagine you had to choose between having $500,000 in the bank and being miserable or having $14,000 in the bank and being content. Which would you

---

[5] This Randy Alcorn book is very detailed and provides a more exhaustive treatment of the subject. In addition, I recommend any book about Biblical stewardship written by Ron Blue.

choose? Affluence without contentment ultimately results in misery.

The exhortation “Give Charitably” only requires that you give something on a regular basis. As you determine an amount to give you may conclude that your immediate needs and goals don’t allow you to give very much. While I sympathize with this, I also know that your needs and goals will continue to expand in the future, and giving money away will always be a sacrifice. Despite what you may think now, getting older or having a higher income will not make charitable giving feel easier.

Remember the clients I described earlier - the generous givers who tend to experience the most financial freedom? They have made a lifetime habit of giving a large percentage of their gross income to charity. Start, as many of these folks did, by giving 10% of your income as a baseline, and then seek ways to increase that percentage over time.

Receiving a bonus may be an opportune time to make one-time gifts, like a year-end gift. Receiving an increase in your salary or hourly rate may be a good time to increase the total percentage of your recurring giving by one or two percent of your gross income.

While giving always comes at an obvious cost to the rest of your budget, strive to give some money away as a habit and continue to evaluate the best level of giving for you. In over 25 years of financial planning, I have never observed a client regret a commitment to giving generously. You will be blessed as you make generosity a habit.

In over 25 years of financial planning, I have never observed a client regret a commitment to giving generously.

Now I am in my fifties. My personal desire to give has expanded along with both my income and my cash flow margins. I still have desires that focus on consumption, but I get much delight in giving and seeing others blessed. I hope you will begin a journey of generosity that will provide you with delight and enjoyment. I am confident you will find the benefits well worth the cost.

Let's pretend that you discover a large pile of French currency early in February 2012 - stacks and stacks of French franc bills. You know the French adopted the Euro as its currency about ten years earlier. As you research a little bit, you realize that the National Bank of France will exchange all French franc bills into valid Euro currency before February 17, 2012, but that the bills will become worthless after February 17.

What do you do?

Knowing the French bills have considerable value now but that they will have no value in the near future, you immediately decide to exchange the soon-to-be-worthless bills for a currency that will have value in the future.

What you and I earn and accumulate now is like the French franc of early 2002. The earnings have value for a limited time, but utility that has a finite shelf life. The challenge for each of us is, "If my money and possessions are useless to me for all eternity after I pass away from this Earth, what is the best use of these resources now?"

Exhortation Two

SET AND TAKE ACTION ON FINANCIAL GOALS

Seventeen frogs sat on a log. Nine decided to jump off.[6]

△ △ △ △ △ △

What do you really want to accomplish with your money? If you could only accomplish one or two things financially, what would they be? These questions call you to identify desired future outcomes; pondering these questions and identifying what you really value will serve you well. Pondering these questions and changing your behavior, as needed, will serve you even better.

Goal setting is not a one-time event. It is a process that requires you to regularly revisit your desires and circumstances. Identifying financial goals is an important step toward making financial progress. Your goals may be locked in right now and you, together with your spouse if you are married, may have great clarity on what they are. When you are in your twenties, thinking

---

[6] The "Frog Riddle" is a common old riddle. It is certainly not mine - even though I repeat it often.

ten years in the future (let alone forty) can be difficult and you may not have thought much about long-term financial goals. If you haven't started thinking of this yet, start now.

Identify Your Goals

You might consider these short-term goals as very important:

- Charitable giving
- Building and maintaining an emergency fund
- Building cash for a major purchase like a car
- Organizing spending to be able to live on one income
- Eliminating smaller debts like credit cards, auto, student loans, etc.

You might consider some of these long-term financial goals:

- Purchasing a home and setting a desired debt-free date on the mortgage
- Retiring all debt by a certain age
- Building wealth or saving for retirement
- Paying for a state-school equivalent college education for any future children (or even half of it!)
- Preparing to care financially for parents or other family, as needed

Other goals and objectives that you are excited about may come to mind; this is an ongoing list that is specific to you.[7]

Let's review each of the common goals and desires listed above.

---

[7] You might list "get a new will executed," "be current on all your payments," or "maintain adequate life insurance" as financial goals, too, but these items may be more appropriate as items on a to-do list. By all means, put these on a list, address them, and get them done. If you prefer to call these goals, get them done in the next two weeks and mark them off as completed.

Common Short-term Financial Goals

- ***Some level of charitable giving.*** Consistent with my personal conviction to give 10% or more of my gross income, many people express a conviction to give to charity based on their income. Giving to charity affects your cash flow, so identifying any giving convictions you have is important. As you reflect on your desires regarding giving, quantify these desires into a concrete goal. Plan to revisit this decision regularly. ***Context:*** Most often, faith-based conviction giving is expressed as a percentage of income, but not always.

- ***Building and maintaining an emergency fund.*** Financial planning textbooks say that you want to keep three to six months of your debt payments and lifestyle spending in an emergency fund. These funds can help provide some breathing room if your income unexpectedly drops due to illness, short-term disability, or loss of job. Some factors can make a smaller (or larger) emergency fund appropriate. It is important to identify the desired balance for your emergency fund, especially if you are starting from zero and not currently committing savings to this on a monthly basis. ***Context:*** Common financial planning wisdom suggests you set aside between three and six months' worth of your current living expenses and debt payments, creating an ideal emergency fund balance of 20% to 40% of your annual gross income.

- ***Building cash for major purchases.*** If you desire to buy and maintain a house or a car, take an extravagant vacation, or pay for braces one day, it would be ideal to prepare for these by building cash reserves over and above your emergency fund. You can see how these items won't fit into your normal monthly budget. Setting cash aside in advance can reduce the likelihood that you are forced to borrow to address these needs when they arise. ***Context:*** The value and age of your house and cars will play a major role in identifying upcoming major purchases.

- ***Organizing spending to be able to live on one income.*** This goal does not always drive a need to create a certain savings balance. Rather, it dictates setting your lifestyle spending at a level that can be maintained by one income. The best way to drive your lifestyle spending down to a certain level may be to simply divert some of your income to savings. Exactly where you place the savings generated from the second income (to make sure it isn't spent) is less important than making sure that the money does not filter down to your checking account where it can more easily appear to be available for everyday use. ***Context:*** Limiting spending to fit into one income will create significant cash flow margin while you still have two incomes.

- ***Paying off smaller loans.*** This usually includes the elimination of student loans, car loans, credit card debt, or sometimes family loans.[8] People often express a desire to eliminate smaller loans to free up the cash that is currently devoted to that payment. Paying off a car loan, for example, can free up cash that can be saved for your next car purchase. The more cash saved for the next car purchase, the less dependent on debt you may be for that purchase. ***Context:*** Eliminating $200 in monthly loan payments can allow you to save $5,000 in just over two

[8] Don't be confused by ads for personal loans that say, "Eliminate all those high-interest loans with a new personal loan from our Company." You are not eliminating any debt by consolidating or refinancing! You are simply rearranging your debt.

years if you don't start spending the 'old loan payment' once the debt is retired.

Common Long-term Financial Goals

- ***Purchasing a home and setting a desired debt-free date.*** Homeownership is both daunting and scary. Does any single financial decision say permanency and responsibility more clearly than buying a home? Owning and maintaining a home is both a long-term commitment and expensive, but you will always live somewhere. Owning a home can be rewarding, provide great family memories, and eventually become the cheapest place to live (once there is no longer a mortgage, that is). When you buy your first home, deciding on a specific future date when you desire to fully own a home with no mortgage is a great start. Setting a debt-free date for your home purchase will help you avoid serially buying a new home (or refinancing your first home) with a new 30-year mortgage. Continuing to use 30-year mortgages will certainly keep you in debt so much longer![9] ***Context:*** When you borrow $250,000 on a 30-year mortgage at 5%, you end up paying over $233,140 in interest and $250,000 in principle over the life of the loan.

- ***Retiring debts by certain dates.*** Paying the minimum on student loans, car loans, and credit card debts will keep you current on the loan schedules. Decide now, though, when you would like to have all these debts eliminated.

---

[9] Starting over with a new 30-year mortgage each time may let you buy more house each time. You want to buy more house when it fits into your desired debt-free date rather than extending your debt-free date every time you add to your existing debt. Otherwise, you may accidentally be 63 (in a nice house) but owe $280,000 on a house valued at $400,000 – when the purchase price of your first home was $95,000. I've seen it happen.

This requires you to decide how important retiring this debt is compared to enjoying lifestyle spending today. If you decide you can live with the debt (and the debt payments) for the duration of the loan term that is fine – but acknowledge it and recognize how this will continue to affect your future cash flow. Remember that your current debt payments require you to devote future cash flow to pay for these - and this limits future margin. ***Context:*** Advertisers and lenders want to convince you that 'being able to afford the monthly payment' is the same as being able to responsibly buy something.

- ***Saving for retirement.*** Time is a big deal for all goals; the sooner you start, the easier it is to accumulate. It is hard to deny current needs and desires because they seem so pressing right now! Maximizing employer-matching contributions is essential. ***Context:*** Investing $4,000 annually from age 25 to age 65 with an 8% annual return will generate a balance of over $1,200,000 at age 65. Increase the contribution from $4,000 to $6,000 every year and the balance at age 65 grows to over $1,800,000 at age 65.[10]

- ***Saving for education for children.*** If you value higher education and want to be prepared to pay for some or all post-high school education for your children, you should start investing early for this goal if you can. ***Context:*** If college costs rise at 5% per year, and you desire to pay for 50% of the four-year cost to attend the state university, you *need to invest about $2,850 per year starting at your child's birth as long as you can earn 7% annually on your investments.*[11] If you wait until your

---

[10] See Appendix 2 for more details on these calculations.

[11] This assumes you want to pay the future equivalent of $12,500 per year for college. Today $12,500 pays for about half a year of a state

child starts 1st Grade, the required annual investment rises from $2,850 to $5,475 per year to pay for the same college education.[12]

- ***Prepare to care financially for parents or other family members.*** The financial costs of assisting aging parents can be very expensive and, therefore, preparing for it can be difficult. Because the non-financial cost of assisting an aging relative can be so draining, having the flexibility to help financially becomes very important to some people. ***Context:*** Currently, the typical hourly cost for a home healthcare worker in North Carolina can approach $20 per hour. If assistance was needed 14 hours a day and seven days a week, the weekly costs would rise to almost $2,000 per week. Even modest retirement living facilities can cost anywhere from $3,000 to $8,000 per month depending on the level of medical care that is needed.[13]

All of your goals are important to you, but you are not equally passionate about each of them. Consider how important each goal is to you and prioritize your income to make progress on the most important goals first. Sorting and labeling your goals based on their relative importance will allow you to take action to accomplish them.

---

school college cost. Note that investing $2,850 annually requires about $237 per month in investments.

[12] The $5,475 per year, or about $456 per month will provide enough assets (with 7% annual growth) to pay for the same education you can get in 2023 for $12,500 with 5% annual inflation. Waiting from birth to 1st Grade to start investing for college is a very expensive proposition!

[13] The monthly cost of retirement living facilities is very complex, some of these facilities require 'buy-ins' that can range from $0 to as high as several hundred thousand dollars. As you might expect, the nicest, cleanest, most modern facilities cost the most.

Sorting and Labeling Your Financial Goals

Some of your goals are extremely important and you have great resolve to accomplish them. Other goals are very important to you, and you will sacrifice to accomplish them. Other goals on your radar screen are more aspirational in nature, and you hope you can one day achieve them. Categorizing each goal based on its importance is helpful.

My Dad ("Boppy" to his grandchildren in their twenties) was quite a distance runner back in the day. He won first place overall in several local road races and completed multiple marathons. While I was in high school, Boppy set a goal to run at least one mile every day and did so for 995 straight days.[14]

Running one mile, for a reasonably healthy person, is not that hard. Running at least one mile a day, *every day,* takes ***incredible resolve***. Have you ever done anything for 995 days in a row? Boppy was very committed, and he did not let any obstacle get in his way. Rainy days, snowy days, cold days, days he didn't feel well, travel days – nothing deterred him. We tend to find all kinds of reasons to explain why something can't get done. For 995 days in a row, Boppy gave no excuses and ran at least one mile every day!

Next, picture my mother-in-law ("Grammy" to her grandchildren in their twenties) fixing dinner at Thanksgiving. She set the expectation that dinner would be served at 5 PM. She intended to serve dinner at 5 PM, and she worked very hard to do it. Invariably, with eighteen loved ones in the house and about fifteen separate dishes to prepare, we usually had our dinner after 5 PM.

Grammy worked incredibly hard to serve last Thanksgiving's dinner at 5 PM. This posed a dilemma for Grammy because, while she valued the goal of eating at 5 PM, she also valued getting

---

[14] Boppy had to end his streak because he was hospitalized for surgery. The surgery was not related to his running.

everyone's drink order just right (with or without ice), helping the youngest get a taste of the fruit salad before everyone else, and using the microwave to warm the empty dinner plates for Grandaddy. Ultimately, her 'goal' to care for her family triumphed over serving dinner at precisely 5 PM. She wanted to reach her goal of 5 PM, and she made great efforts to reach it, but she ultimately had to choose between competing priorities; a delicious meal was eaten just after 5 PM.

The final image to picture is me eating a second helping of chips from my favorite Mexican restaurant. They are so good, and they have a seemingly magical ability to soften the hard edges of even the hardest day. They are an escape. Picture me enjoying these chips as I proclaim, "I want to lose 15 pounds!"

My recurring resolution to lose weight has often fallen victim to tortilla chips. In fact, you might remember me making the same resolution last year (and the year before that), but that was five "free-entrees-through-the-loyalty-program" ago. The noble goal of losing weight has often been a sincerely desired outcome, but it was not a priority that frequently dictated my behavior to change. In that sense, it was not really a goal at all– though I may have used that word. It was really just a wish. I wish I could lose weight while still eating the types and quantities of food I want.

Goals that do not dictate any behavioral changes are not really goals. They are just wishes.

So, you have Boppy's resolve to run one mile a day dictating decisions in almost every aspect of his daily and weekly schedule for almost three years. You have Grammy who wanted to serve dinner at 5 PM, but she made other decisions along the way that revealed that she valued other things too. She worked hard to get dinner served at 5 PM, but not at all costs. Finally, you have me proclaiming one thing is very important but simultaneously being unwilling to follow through on any sacrifices required to accomplish the ultimate goal.

Going forward, you can use these three images as a reference for how you want to approach your goals. The approach will reveal the type of conviction you have regarding the goal. Some of your goals may be '1-mile-a-day' goals, some may be 'Eat-at-5-PM' goals, and others will be 'Tortilla Chip' goals. You may immediately identify with all three of these types. They may each fit an area of your life – and you might be able to identify some financial goals that fit into one or more.

If you don't intentionally identify any goals, you *will still* prioritize your spending. That is, you *will still choose* to spend or save for some things over others every day and every month. You will likely be reactionary and will not make coordinated progress toward any particular longer-term goals. This may not lead to deep regret down the road, but your fifty-year-old self will likely wonder why you did not make faster progress.

The sooner you can identify your '1-mile-a-day' and your 'Eat-at-5-PM' goals, the better. Timing means so very much, as we will discuss next.

Goals and Time

You acquire a dollar. You can only use that dollar once.

If you spend it, it is gone. If you give it away, it is gone. If you borrowed in the past and have debts to pay now, you spent that dollar in the past. If you save or invest it, you can use that dollar (and any associated gains or losses) in the future. Any way you look at it, you can only use it once.

A budget, at its very essence, is an allocation of how much of your income you've ***already spent*** (your debt payments), how much of your income you will ***spend right now*** for immediate needs, and how much of your income you will choose to ***spend in the future***.

When you make a debt payment, you are spending today's income on money you've already spent. When you pay for insurance, taxes, and all lifestyle spending, you are spending money on things you are using right now. When you save or invest money, you are preparing to spend that money in the future.

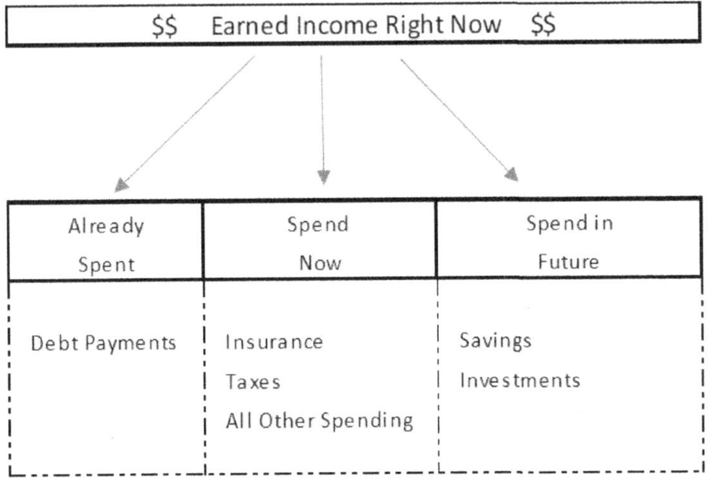

How do you begin to appreciate the urgency of a distant goal? What would make you want to be able to spend the money you earn today in the future?

The actual attainment of your goals will undoubtedly require you to spend more money than you earn in certain time periods. Common reasons people spend significantly more money than they earn in a given time period include:

- Education - The need to spend more than your current income is common for future educational expenses. It is hard to fit private school costs or college costs in a regular monthly budget.
- Home or Car Purchase and Maintenance - Major home expenses like roof repairs, HVAC replacements, painting, water heaters, etc. don't fit in a monthly budget. Car

purchases, new tires, regular car maintenance and repairs can be hard to fit into your regular annual budget.

- Medical Costs - Health related costs can easily drive you to spend more in one year than you make. Some of these costs are known and can be planned for, but others present themselves at inconvenient times whether you have saved for them or not.
- Retirement - Anything you would like to spend money on after you stop working will require you to spend more money than you make.[15] Sometimes people stop working voluntarily, and sometimes it is involuntary, but planned retirement is the obvious one here.
- Other Reasons - "Wedding, wedding, and wedding," says the father of three girls. True, societal norms and other people's expectations do not have to dictate how much you spend on something like a wedding, but you will run into other needs and desires that exceed your annual available cash flow. Landscaping, an anniversary trip, braces - things will come up!

Many of these types of expenses, while the exact timing and amounts are unpredictable, are natural consequences of choices made. For example, having a roof and an HVAC unit in your house or owning an automobile for transportation will bring up rather expensive maintenance and replacement costs from time to time. Many of these examples are great reasons for an emergency fund and savings set aside for major purchases, but the future cost to maintain or replace many of these items will cause you to spend more in a year than you make.

Also, know that there will be things you want to pay for after you stop working that you can't identify right now. You probably should not trust yourself to think, "If I can't think of it and understand its future significance to me and my family right now,

---

[15] True - you may receive Social Security Retirement benefits after you stop working. This income does help. It is a hard life, though, to meet all of your needs in retirement using only this monthly income.

then I won't regret not preparing for it." Whether you see the value of preparing for future expenses or you are blind to them, these future expenses will exist and preparing for these will be a blessing to you.

So, let's concede that you have the desire to have some dollars available to spend when you won't have enough income for them in the future. This is true if you can identify why, as in "I want to retire at age 65." But it is also true if you can't identify the exact reason, as in "I am 64 and haven't saved a dime. What comes next for me?" There are three main factors that will determine how much money you will have available for future needs:

1. How many of your 'earlier-earned' dollars did you set aside for this purpose?
2. At what rate did your invested dollars grow?
3. When did you set the money aside?

The first two items are fairly simple. The third item is, by far, the most significant. That's where you, as a person in your twenties, find opportunity. It really is all about ***time***.

Let's assume you have 12 months to prepare for a $10,000 purchase. We will assume you can earn an 8% return on any money you invest. Here are three ways you can prepare for this purchase:

- Early - You can set money aside right now, 12 months ahead of time.
- Delayed - You can set money aside in six months at the halfway point.
- Late - You can set the money aside at the very last minute.

Strategy	Total at end of 12 Months	Total Investment Gain at 8%*	Total Investment Required
Set money aside at beginning - *Early*	$10,000	$766	$9,234
Set money aside halfway - *Delayed*	$10,000	$391	$9,609
Set money aside at end - *Waited*	$10,000	$0	$10,000

* 8% annual gain is illustrated and taxes are ignored.

Each of the three strategies provides the desired $10,000 at the appropriate time, but look at the results in the far-right column in the table above. As you probably expected, the strategy that started earliest was able to create $10,000 by investing fewer dollars than the other two strategies which started later.

The difference may be more dramatic than you may think. The early starter used only $9,234 of cash from cash flow[16] to create $10,000 twelve months later. The delayed starter must save over $300 more than the early starter, requiring $9,609 to be used from cash flow to create the $10,000. The late starter had to pull the full $10,000 out of cash flow.

The early start creates a significant cash flow difference!

If you are not yet convinced that time is an investor's best friend, consider this: If your goal was to accumulate $500,000 by your 66th birthday by earning 8% annually, here is how much you must invest monthly based on your starting age:

Monthly Investment Contribution Required to Accumulate $500,000 by Your 66th Birthday with 8% Gains		
Starting Birthday	Required Monthly Investment	# of Monthly Contributions
25	$131	492
30	$199	432
35	$306	372
40	$477	312
45	$764	252
50	$1,283	192
55	$2,359	132

So, on your 25th birthday if you invest $131 in an account that grows at 8% every year, and repeat this every month until you turn 66, your investment balance would exceed $500,000 on

[16] Cash flow, for our purposes, includes the decision-making and use of all money you earn, spend, save and invest.

your 66th birthday.[17] Similarly, a 40-year-old needs to begin investing $477 monthly in an investment that returns 8% every year for the investment balance to exceed $500,000 on their 66th birthday.[18]

Can you accumulate $500,000 by age 66 if you are starting at $0 at age 55? Probably not. Especially if your pattern has been to save $0 during your first 55 years! It is just impossible to suddenly have the ability to save $2,359 every month when you have spent every available dollar in the previous 54 years. Can you accumulate $500,000 if you start at age 25? It is much more likely since this 'only' requires $131 per month.

It is certainly easier to build asset balances if you start early. Even postponing regular investments from age 25 to age 30 increases the monthly required investment from $131 to $199. This $68 increase applies to 432 monthly contributions until your 66th birthday. Investing $199 requires 52% more money than the $131 monthly investment that a 25-year-old requires. No matter your current age or your desired ending investment account value, the earlier you start the easier it is!

> No matter your current age or your desired ending investment account value – the earlier you start the easier it is!

Many will say at age 25, "I am just starting, and I have other important needs like saving for a car, building an emergency fund, and paying for my own car insurance. I just can't save for this, too. I'll start in a few years when my income is higher." Keeping it real, here: If you are unwilling or unable to commit $131 a month to retirement at age 25, you will find it

[17] The 25-year-old makes 492 monthly investments of $131 over 41 years. This is a total of $64,452 invested.

[18] The 40-year-old makes 312 monthly investments of $477 over 26 years. This is a total of $148,824 invested. (See how much better it is to be 25 than 40?)

incredibly difficult to commit $199 per month to retirement starting at age 30 - no matter how much your income rises. Even if you cannot invest your desired amount today, start by investing some amount and then seek to increase the amount every time your income rises.

So, where does this leave us? If you are like most, you have virtually unlimited desires, but you have limited resources. This is what makes financial decision-making so hard! If you didn't have future desires (or future needs that will come whether you desire them or not), you could spend all your money on today. *Stewardship is the responsibility to navigate through life with virtually unlimited needs and desires with limited resources.* No one said it would be easy.

That is why a careful and thoughtful reflection on your most important needs and desires is where you start. That is why you need to identify and prioritize your goals. What is most important to you? Setting meaningful personal goals helps you prioritize where your money goes.

Early identification allows time to be your friend instead of your enemy. The sooner you identify and prioritize your goals, and the sooner you start applying some of your current income to future needs, the easier progress will become. And, hey, the progress is for you to make towards ***your*** goals – what ***you*** have convictions about – not what interests your friends, co-workers, peers, or even your family. This *is about you and your financial convictions.*

- If you want to live in a smaller house because it allows you to pay for a private school, do it.
- If you want to save for college, do it.
- If you want to retire at age 60, do it.
- If you want to be debt-free by age 45, do it.

And, if you want to use your current income to maximize your current spending and make no preparation for any future goals, do it. But don't be surprised by future outcomes that may be disappointing. This is obviously not the recommended path.

Realizing at age 65 that retirement at age 70 will require you to significantly reduce your lifestyle spending patterns is tough for people to digest.[19] Most retired folks have fairly simple desires.

- They want to have access to good medical care.
- They want to make housing choices for non-financial reasons.
- They want to travel to see grandchildren.
- They don't want to be a financial burden to their children.

Accumulating sufficient financial resources can give them the confidence and peace of mind to accomplish and enjoy these desires. Failing to think ahead and prepare financially is limiting and disappointing to many.

Humanly speaking, you and your decisions are the biggest determinants of your future financial outcomes.

Humanly speaking, you and your decisions are the biggest determinants of your future financial outcomes.[20] The sooner your behavior reflects this, the better off you will be. Identifying your financial goals early is a very important first step and beginning to take action is crucial.

Timing matters.

[19] Again, to be sure – you don't need to fund a retirement that is extravagant and meets anyone else's expectations. There is nothing morally or spiritually superior about someone who has saved more. People can and do make idols out of investment balances.

[20] Even if you hold fast to strong faith convictions and trust in both God's sovereignty and His providence, your actions will be the biggest single factor in determining your financial outcomes. God will likely use both financial blessing and financial hardship in various seasons of your life. May you find joy in accomplishing desires and learn perseverance as you see some earthly desires deferred.

I had several '1-mile-a-day' goals in my twenties. My personal experience may help you begin to see and understand how specific goals can influence and dictate other financial decisions.

Goals from my Twenties

In my twenties, I developed strong convictions regarding four specific cash flow goals. Each of these goals was a '1-mile-a-day' goal and dictated what money was available for all other spending.

Three *short-term* goals drove my decision-making on monthly spending. These were as follows:

- Giving away a minimum of 10% of gross income
- Investing enough in retirement to maximize the company matching contribution
- Limiting total spending to allow our family to meet all spending needs on just one income

Both the giving and investing goals listed above are fairly straightforward; the third deserves some elaboration.

Though my wife was a trained and experienced educator, she and I had complete unity on a desire for her to stay home full-time with any young children we had. We agreed that this was the best way for her to use not only her skills and training but also her giftedness to love and nurture people. I understand that this is not everyone's desire. We believed this was best for our family, so we prioritized our lifestyle expenses to make this possible.[21]

Accordingly, we began building a budget that allowed my income to cover all our past and current needs. We knew that we could support our monthly budget on one income if we were able to

---

[21] I acknowledge that some financial circumstances don't allow for one parent to stay home with children. I do think, though, there are many who say they can't afford it, but they actually could if they really valued it most and were willing to reduce lifestyle spending.

use 100% of the second income on things we were willing to eliminate when we dropped to one income.

For example, the second income may have been allocated as follows:

- 10% Giving
- 20% Income and Payroll Taxes
- 25% Savings (for a Major Purchase fund)
- 20% Savings for a 5th Anniversary Vacation
- 25% Investment in retirement

Using the second income in this fashion allowed us to give generously, pay taxes, and build more savings and investments. Most importantly, we were not relying on this income for parts of our budget that we could not bear to cut.

As you can tell we also made great progress by building cash reserves and building retirement assets. This was motivating to us because we knew our ability to save and invest in the future would be much smaller after dropping to one income. Regardless of exactly how (or even why) we allocated the second income the way we did, the important decision was to structure the use of the second income so that we could go without spending any of the second income on necessary, recurring items.

If we had not been diligent and disciplined in using the second income like this for several years before our children arrived, I might have falsely concluded, "I would like for Mommy to stay home, but we just can't afford it."

If you are thinking, "I am not sure what I will want to do workwise if I am able to have, or adopt, a child." It is valuable to begin analyzing the uses of the second income now and, over time, build a family budget that allows you to use the second income for things that you can run your household without; even if this just means you are primarily stockpiling retirement investments, an emergency fund, money for your next car, or money to pay down debt faster.

Stashing a large portion of the second income into savings and investments will prove beneficial down the road. If you later decide that you will continue to have two incomes rather than one, you will not regret having used the second income for these future needs and giving yourself the financial freedom to get by on one income.

To gauge the distance you are from being able to run your household on one income, you can simply determine what percentage of the second income is needed for lifestyle desires. If you are still relying on 50% of the second income for desired lifestyle spending, you still have a considerable way to go. The smaller the percentage of the second income that is necessary for lifestyle spending, the closer you are to having the freedom to drop your income without sacrificing your lifestyle spending. This means you also have a greater percentage of the second income going towards convictions and margin, and that helps make financial progress!

You can see how these three short-term '1-mile-a-day' goals shaped my cash flow. The giving was done as a percentage of income every time I got paid. Retirement contributions were made on my paystub to maximize the company matching contribution. Finally, lifestyle spending was analyzed and limited to fit within the available cash flow derived from my income alone. These goals were so important that they dictated other spending choices I made.

How much should I spend on vacation or at Christmas? Which lawnmower should I buy? What house should I rent (or buy)? Do I repair the car or replace it? All of these decisions were made in light of the commitment to give, invest in retirement, and build a sustainable budget that could be maintained on one income. The goals dictated spending decisions in all other areas, not the other way around. *This did require intentionality.* If I had not made a conscious effort to address the three short-term goals first, I would have made everyday lifestyle spending decisions and then would have addressed the three goals with whatever was left over. Do you see the difference between being intentional and reactive?

These three short-term goals provided boundaries rooted in conviction. I chose to run '1-mile-a-day', and then I planned the rest of my schedule.

My number one *long-term* goal in my twenties was to organize my cash flow to allow myself to be completely debt-free before my first child would start college.[22] This goal became a primary driver in monthly cash flow decisions going forward, but the real impetus for this goal was the longer-term effect.

In 1994, during pre-marital counseling sessions, my fiancé and I decided on this primary long-term financial goal. This goal drove our decision-making for over 20 years and served as a great blessing to our marriage and our family. The anticipated benefits of being debt-free were very compelling. We were always able to use our goal to calculate and prioritize cash flow as we aged and were faced with other financial choices. Effective goal setting usually includes specific and measurable goals. In our case, at age 24, this goal was not perfect. We had no children (nor any guarantee of any), which meant we had no target date to focus on. Additionally, we had no debt at the time. What we got was this – a goal, in principle, that would shape and dictate future decisions regarding our lifestyle spending and housing decisions. We could evaluate these decisions in light of how they made the achievement of our debt retirement goal more or less likely. Eventually, after the birth of our first child, we could quantify the target date for being debt-free.

---

[22] I am using "I" in the singular, but financial decisions made once engaged and married were always done in conjunction with, and in unity with, my wife. We didn't always agree on everything (of course), but we sought, worked for and achieved unity on all major goals and financial decisions.

There was still so much uncertainty. How would my income change over the next 20 years? How would our lifestyle needs and desires change if more children came along? Despite the future uncertainty, we agreed. It is worth the work to identify the goals that excite you, and then begin working towards them.

The debt-free goal excited me because we knew we would have greater freedom to give and spend later in life if we had no debt. We would also have greater freedom to use cash flow to pay for college if we had no debt. So, in a way, our debt-retirement goal was also a college savings goal. We do value education very highly. The elimination of debt contributed to paying for college in the same way that investing for college would have contributed. Ultimately, financial goals are interrelated, even when they seem very different.

As we considered a home purchase, our goal of being debt-free by September 2016 provided a framework to evaluate both how much we should spend on a house and how aggressively we should strive to pay down the debt. Many people make housing decisions with other good questions at the top of their minds:

- Will this house appreciate in value?
- Is this the best school district for our kids?
- Is the neighborhood nice enough?
- What will others think of us if we live in this neighborhood?
- What maintenance expenses are likely in the first five years if we buy this house?
- Can we stretch to afford the mortgage payment in the early years?
- Will this purchase decision create undue pressure to maximize income – even if the work requirements to maintain that income may harm the health of our marriage or family?
- Will living in this neighborhood exert subtle pressure on us to upgrade our cars sooner and maintain other costly appearances?

- Are we presuming too much about the future by taking on this debt?

Because our goal was about paying off the house, not just buying it, our focus was not just on acquiring the house but retiring the debt. Our main question was, "How does buying this house, with this mortgage, affect our ability to be debt-free by September 2016?"

In addition to being debt-free, I had other financial goals, too. As a result, I did invest some money for higher education to take advantage of years of compounding. I also invested in retirement funds as I've mentioned.

In some ways, the goal to be debt-free before our child starts college was a '1-mile-a-day' goal. In other ways, it was an 'Eat-at-5-PM' goal. We had great conviction about this goal, and it drove many of our decisions. We did do some balancing with other goals and lifestyle desires, however, in large part due to my variable income.

Final Thoughts on Goals

Making financial decisions is hard. The process of identifying your goals and prioritizing your spending is valuable. You will find more satisfaction from the process and its result than living responsively to life's events.

Setting goals is good. Taking action is good. Taking action demonstrates that you are really committed to running '1-mile-a-day'. Working hard and striving to accomplish what you believe are the right things to do. Humanly speaking, you and your choices are the biggest determinants of your financial outcomes.

This is not revolutionary thinking; it is common sense. Wisdom literature from the Bible reinforces this.

> *Go to the ant, O sluggard; consider her ways, and be wise. Without having any chief, officer, or ruler, she prepares her bread in summer and gathers her food in*

> *harvest. How long will you lie there, O sluggard? When will you arise from your sleep? A little sleep, a little slumber, a little folding of the hands to rest, and poverty will come upon you like a robber, and want like an armed man.* **Proverbs 6:6–11**
>
> *The plans of the diligent lead surely to abundance, but everyone who is hasty comes only to poverty.* **Proverbs 21:5**
>
> *Every prudent man acts with knowledge, but a fool flaunts his folly.* **Proverbs 13:16**
>
> *Know well the condition of your flocks, and give attention to your herds...* **Proverbs 27:23**
>
> *So teach us to number our days that we may get a heart of wisdom.* **Psalm 90:12**

Jesus himself asked in Luke 14:28, "For which of you, desiring to build a tower, does not first sit down and count the cost, whether he has enough to complete it?"

While you and your actions are, humanly speaking, the biggest determinant of your financial future, this does not mean that you can dictate all the outcomes. Results are not guaranteed. You cannot simply muster enough willpower and self-discipline to achieve whatever you desire; you may find that you have competing goals that cannot be accomplished at the same time.[23] You may prioritize some non-financial goals as more important than financial goals.[24] In addition, there are forces outside of your control that will be obstacles that create failure.

---

[23] For example, you may want to save $250 a month in savings AND also pay down a car loan with an extra $250 each month, but you may only have $350 of cash flow available.

[24] You may choose to drop down to one income for a time, even if this means you contribute less to retirement.

These challenges should not be unexpected. As I reflect on other parts of wisdom literature, this makes sense.

> *The heart of man plans his way, but the LORD establishes his steps.* **Proverbs 16:9**
>
> *Many are the plans in the mind of a man, but it is the purpose of the LORD that will stand.* **Proverbs 19:21**
>
> *Come now, you who say, "Today or tomorrow we will go into such and such a town and spend a year there and trade and make a profit"— yet you do not know what tomorrow will bring. What is your life? For you are a mist that appears for a little time and then vanishes. Instead you ought to say, "If the Lord wills, we will live and do this or that." As it is, you boast in your arrogance. All such boasting is evil.* **James 4:13–16**

These are good reminders about the importance of prayer because, ultimately, there is so little we can control.

Let's get back to the seventeen frogs that sat on a log. Nine decided to jump off. How many frogs are on the log?

Many people confidently say, "Eight."

> …there is a difference between deciding to and actually doing…

This is actually a snarky little illustration that may explain why many people want to make financial progress but frequently don't. There are still seventeen frogs on that log because there is a difference between deciding and actually doing.[25] When you develop a

[25] Again, this common old "Frog Riddle" supplies the moral of the story. Not an original, but I wish it was.

'1-mile-a-day' goal, you don't want something that is less important to jeopardize progress towards this goal.

Begin to think about the jumping you will start doing. You need to identify the goals and desires you have that are '1-mile-a-Day' goals and you need to identify which are 'Eat-at-5-PM' goals. If you are treating some goals like 'Tortilla Chip' goals, don't expect progress. Take action and have your goals dictate your financial decisions!

Exhortation Three

CREATE MARGIN

Crowders Mountain in Kings Mountain, North Carolina, sits about twenty-five miles west of Charlotte. From its peak on a clear day, you can see Charlotte's skyline. Imagine standing there, taking a popsicle stick in your hand, holding it upright, and extending your arm toward Charlotte in the east. You will notice that the popsicle stick appears to be overwhelmingly taller than the tallest building on the skyline. It is, in fact, not larger than *any* building in Charlotte, let alone the tallest building which is sixty stories high at a height of just over 870 feet. Still, the popsicle stick *seems* to be larger than the tallest building in the state of North Carolina.

△ △ △ △ △ △

A typical timeline for a wage-earning person looks like this:

0	22	67	87
Birth	Work	Retire	Die

For the first twenty-two years or so, you are generally dependent on and supported by others. You then begin working, and perhaps caring for other dependents, for about forty-five years.

During these forty-five years, in addition to making ends meet, you might buy a house and raise and educate children. You also have to prudently save money to fund your retirement for twenty years after you stop working; a less-than-100-year-old American invention called 'retirement'.

To complicate things, during your 45 working years, you will find pressing and timely urges to take nice vacations, buy nice (and/or reliable) cars, enjoy the latest fashions and phones, and maintain the appearance of not being less successful than your friends, families, neighbors, and peers.

So, how do you make all this work? The special sauce is to *create margin*. Be committed to creating margin right now and keep on doing it.

You simply cannot achieve long-term goals without creating margin. Unless you are satisfied to live with constant financial strain and anxiety or to teeter on the edge of bankruptcy, you must be willing to not spend all your money![26]

Margin is money you earn now that is saved or invested for future expenses. This is money from your earned income that is not given away, paid in taxes, paid for rent, paid for debt payments, paid for insurance, or spent on lifestyle spending. You can create margin by saving or investing your earned income; simple to state and simple to understand, but oh, so hard to do.

Creating margin is hard. Few people do it. If you don't believe me, do a web search on "Average Household Debt in the US." You will find that, despite unprecedented wealth and prosperity in our country, Americans at every income level spend more than they make. They do this by borrowing for college, cars, houses, and everyday expenses.

---

[26] Some may say, "Just live by faith and don't get so worked up about this." You should get worked up about this – and so should the naysayer – because your effort here is to make sure you spend your resources on those things that are most important to you.

Incurring debt today commits you to use a portion of your future income to pay for things you have already purchased. As a result, debt makes it harder to make your future income cover all your future expenses. Having to commit any portion of your current income to past purchases (even when purchased at a low-interest rate, or even 0% interest) leaves fewer dollars available for current and future needs.

If you ever want to accumulate any money at all, you have to begin with an initial investment, and you also need to continue making deposits to the investment to expect it to grow in any meaningful way.[27]

To retire one day, you will need to keep on paying for things while you are not earning anything. At present, the US Social Security System can provide a certain amount of retirement income, but likely not enough to support most couples for twenty years in retirement at the lifestyle level with which they are comfortable.

You must pack a lot of savings into your forty-five working years to provide any kind of flexibility for retirement. Sadly, most people who say they really want to retire have not prepared for it.

Many believe that a higher future income will solve long-term financial problems and allow people to reach their goals. You would think this is true, but my professional experience has shown me that more income does not correlate with more margin.[28] The most important thing you can do to create successful financial outcomes is to begin and remain committed

---

[27] Proverbs 13:11 says, "He who makes money little by little, makes it grow."

[28] You can certainly say that higher income correlates with higher spending. But don't automatically think that an increase in income from $80,000 to $100,000 will provide more margin – it does not happen unless you make it happen – and it is hard to do!

to spending less than you earn. *Begin creating margin and keep creating margin.*

Major Elements of your Cash Flow

As we have seen, most people spend all their income – or more. It takes a very intentional effort to create margin. Let's look at the key components of your cash flow to understand what is required to create margin.

Cash Flow In — Gross Income

It is best to orient your thinking around your gross pay and to think of your cash flow on a monthly, or even annual basis. Gross income is the grand total of all cash paid to you. Many people begin to think of their cash flow by starting with their net income that is deposited in their bank account from their paycheck every two weeks or so. By starting with your gross income, you will properly account for expenses that are placed on your paycheck.

As an example, if you have gross monthly income of $5,000, your monthly paycheck may include several deductions like this:

Gross Pay	5,000
Less: Deductions	
Retire: 401k	(300)
Tax: Payroll	(383)
Tax: Federal Income	(376)
Tax: State Income	(235)
Insurance: Health	(125)
Net Pay	3,581

As you can see, there is quite a difference between $5,000 of gross pay and $3,581 net pay.

You may naturally think of, and understand, your cash flow on a per-pay-period basis, but I suggest you analyze your pay on a monthly basis. To 'monthlize' your gross income, you have to convert the gross income on a paycheck to an average monthly gross income.[29]

If you have a two-income household, things become quite confusing very quickly – especially if you are paid at different times and at different intervals. Make the effort to structure your cash flow planning on a monthly basis first.

Simply stated, your income is your gross pay. Even if it seems overwhelming to figure out what your gross pay is on a monthly or annual basis, put in the effort. You can do it!

Cash Flow Out — Three Broad Categories

In the paycheck example above, it was easy to see a sizable number of payroll deductions paid before you received your paycheck. One primary hindrance to good cash flow understanding is the challenge of timing. No matter your job, you will pay for some things out of your gross pay before receiving any money.

This creates a difference between the priorities you place on your spending and the sequencing of paying for them. As you can see in the earlier example, you have made a retirement contribution, paid payroll and income taxes, and paid for health insurance before you ever got a chance to give or invest (or even eat!). It will be helpful to ignore, for the moment anyway, the chronology of these expenses and consider your cash outflow from a broader perspective.

One of the most consequential financial questions you can answer is *"What things should dictate how much we spend on housing and on our recurring lifestyle spending?"* Based on thirty years of empirical evidence, a great number of people under age

---

[29] If you are paid every two weeks, you want to take your gross income from your last paycheck and multiply it by 26, and then divide by twelve. If you are paid twice a month, just multiply your pay stub gross income times 2. If you are paid once a month, there is no conversion needed to arrive at your monthly gross income.

sixty prioritize their spending decisions in a way that they later regret.

What should dictate how much you spend on housing and lifestyle desires? The most common answers a typical person provides would include earned income, personal desires, expectations of others, historical patterns, peer pressure, borrowing capacity, charitable giving desires, and tax levels. That's a lot of "voices" speaking into your personal choices.

Ultimately, your income, your convictions, and your requirements should dictate your spending on housing and your lifestyle spending. We've already described your gross income. Let's examine these three basic spending categories:

- **Convictions** – Your financial convictions include charitable giving and your most important short and long-term financial goals. Each of your '1-mile-a-day' goals belongs here.

- **Requirements** – Your financial requirements will include taxes, debt payments, and appropriate insurance coverage.

Ultimately, your income, your convictions and your requirements should dictate your spending.

- **Lifestyle Spending** – All of your other cash outflow will fall into this category. This includes important items that may technically be 'requirements' like paying your power bill and discretionary items that are more fun like travel, eating out, gifts and vacation.

Will you choose to limit your spending on housing, utilities, entertainment, travel, clothing, and other expenses based on your convictions and requirements? It seems obvious, when stated this way, that you should. But many folks, even if they are not consciously aware of it, will just spend their take-home pay and not realize for a few months (or years) that they have important reasons to create margin; whether they be a car with 240,000 miles with no savings set aside for repairs or replacement, or the future education of a four-year-old. Maybe it is buying a house. Choose today to not become a 58-year-old who has not saved much for retirement, has 18 years left on a mortgage, and has grown accustomed to lifestyle spending that consumes 105% of her earned income.

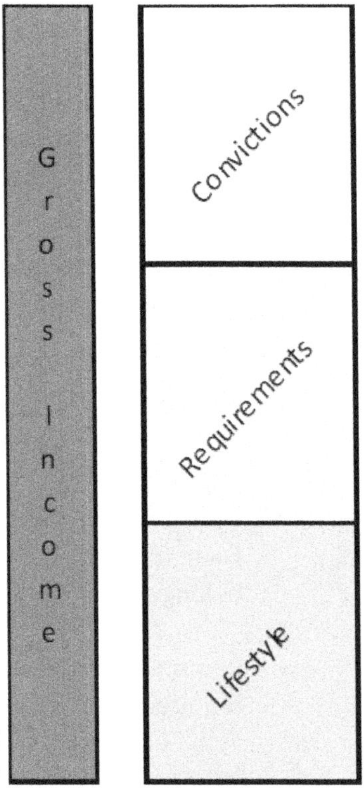

Gross Income

Convictions

Requirements

Lifestyle

Yes, today is the right time to start limiting your housing and lifestyle spending based on your convictions and your requirements. This may cause you to reevaluate your current lifestyle spending – but if this allows you to make faster progress toward ***your***[30] financial goals - the sooner you start, the better. That way, any future adjustments or course corrections will be less difficult to make.

I have seen how the "We-will-just-figure-it-out-later" strategy tends to work out. Sometimes people inherit money at just the right time, but sometimes their parents live too long for an

[30] Don't create margin for me. Don't create it for your parents or your peers. Create the margin to reach your goals.

inheritance to be helpful for certain goals. Sometimes it means working much longer than desired to retire. This notion may seem like a mild inconvenience when you are thirty years old and thinking about a far-off retirement, but it is an entirely different animal when you are sixty-five years old, and you want to travel to (and spoil) grandchildren while your spouse tolerates a bad back and continues to labor at work from age 65 to age 70 'just' to maintain the current lifestyle.

There are many 55-year-olds, who for a variety of reasons, have ended up not saving much money along the way. Some have faced misfortune - like chronic illness, caring for sick relatives, etc. Others have had lifestyle needs that were extraordinarily demanding – six kids, etc. Some have planned poorly; they just went with the flow and seemed to always spend too much to save and lived like they would 'just figure it out' later. For every person/couple in this boat, there are five times as many contributing factors that got them there. I am not judging them. They may not have done anything wrong along the way. But I would guess that each of them would join me in strongly urging you to let your convictions dictate your lifestyle spending and not the other way around – even if you must make sacrifices along the way.

So, how do you identify convictions, requirements and lifestyle desires and begin to apply these to gross income? Let's examine these three types of spending in more detail.

Convictions, Requirements, and Lifestyle Expenses

You will use all your income in one of three ways: convictions, requirements, or lifestyle spending. It is critically important that you address your convictions first, then your requirements, and then your lifestyle spending after that. Reversing this order and organizing your cash flow by starting with your lifestyle spending will create very different long-term outcomes.

Convictions: Giving and Margin

Convictions can be related to '1-mile-a-day' desires of giving or long-term goals like saving, investing, or debt reduction.

As you consider your convictions on giving, you want to focus on what should be done regularly and consistently from your gross income, not just money that appears to be 'leftover'. Of course, you may give additional dollars as needs arise and resources are available, but the giving you do as a first priority is ***conviction giving***. This is the amount (oftentimes a percentage) you want to give as a '1-mile-a-day' goal.

The income that you set aside for first priorities is called the ***conviction margin***. Conviction margin can be categorized as ***conviction savings***, ***conviction investing*** or ***conviction debt reduction*** depending on whether you direct the cash flow to short-term savings, long-term investing, or debt reduction. As mentioned in section two, you can also start to label these goals as '1-mile-a-day' goals and begin applying some of your income to make progress.

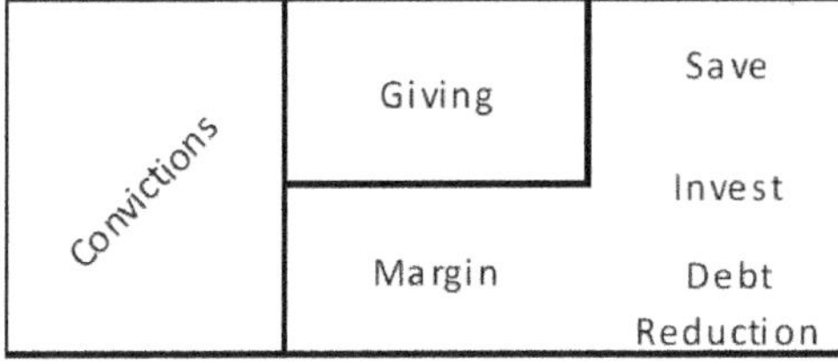

Common examples of short-term, conviction savings include building an emergency fund, saving for a special trip, or preparing for a house or car purchase. You must be realistic about this. It can be tricky, but don't let the unknown variables paralyze you into not starting to make any progress at all.

You will probably experience many major life changes in your twenties. As a result, conviction investing for long-term goals can be easy to ignore because of the urgency of your current needs. This is especially true because so much focus is on short-term desires that seem satisfying or necessary. But you may think twice about spending extravagantly on a really nice vacation if you knew that paying for the vacation today meant you were jeopardizing the achievement of your most important goals in the future. Common examples of long-term goals are retirement, education, or other lifestyle desires that are five or more years in the future.[31]

Like I did in my twenties, you may desire to create conviction margin by accelerating the reduction and eventual elimination of debt. Identifying and acting on conviction debt reduction is common, and it is easily quantifiable if the interest rate on the debt is fixed. Retiring debt can be easy to develop a conviction about, easy to calculate what is required, and easy to make additional monthly payments.

Why is Conviction Margin so Important?

You want to be mindful of the consequences associated with your decisions. Many people pay for unnecessary things today without realizing that paying for these extras now may mean they are unable to afford something else down the road.

Currently, do you have any short-term goals or long-term goals that rise to the level of conviction? Again, it may be difficult to conjure up conviction about providing your child's college in twenty years or about maintaining a certain lifestyle in retirement forty years from now. But what about when your child is seventeen and you desperately want to provide help with a college education? What about when you are sixty-two and you want to stop working and maintain your lifestyle for another 20 years? You want to be prepared for these and the best time to begin preparing is now.

---

[31] Other lifestyle desires that are five or more years in the future may require investment today. These may include a second home purchase, a home upgrade or remodel, a wedding (or three), or other unidentified expenses that you are interested in. If these expenses were short-term in nature, you would use conviction savings to set the money aside.

When you identify goals that are so important they require saving or investing now, you should not just decide they are important; you should build conviction margin into your budget. This means you start adding to your short-term savings, long-term investments or pay extra on your debt. Be a frog that *actually jumps* off the log – not one that just *decides to jump*.

Remember the big picture: you are trying to provide for current (and perhaps future) family needs and save enough to live on for twenty-plus years after you stop working – all in approximately 45 years. This is hard work!

Take steps now to calculate the amount of monthly income that is required to accomplish your conviction margin goals. You may be able to find some helpful resources and calculators online to start this process. If you are unable to calculate how much is required, this may be a great time to consult a financial planner in your area.[32]

One conviction you must develop – if for no other reason than I told you to - is to take full advantage of any company-provided match to a retirement plan.[33] The financial return for you is so compelling that you need to contribute *at least* enough to your company retirement plan to get the full match.

---

[32] Financial planners can help you quantify the progress that sets you on the right trajectory. A very specific investing target can help you define the tangible steps to take to get and stay on track. Look for planners who have the CERTIFIED FINANCIAL PLANNER® certification, and who are fee-only. If it is appealing to have advice from a Biblical framework, consider only Certified Kingdom Advisors.

[33] Companies sometimes offer matching contributions to your retirement account when you elect to have some of your gross pay invested in your retirement account. A typical arrangement is like this: The Company will contribute 50% of what you contribute up to a maximum of 6% of your income. You put in 4% of your pay, they put in 2%. You put in 6%, they put in 3%. You put in 9%, they put in 3%.

Convictions - Putting them into Action

Determine how your '1-mile-a-day' goals will drive you to prioritize both conviction giving and conviction margin. You can always give, save, invest, or pay down debt with additional margin (after your lifestyle spending is done), but first determine how your convictions will dictate the most important use of your income.

Boppy ran one mile when the windchill temperature was minus 20 degrees. He ran on days we drove 500 miles on vacation. He made it happen. He did not let circumstances dictate his ability to run for nine minutes – even when it was very inconvenient and when others thought (knew?) he was a bit crazy. Do you have, or will you develop, any convictions like this?

If you find that you do not have conviction goals at present, consider if that is because it is a new concept to you or if you are unwilling to make giving and future goals a priority. Unwillingness will result in undesirable outcomes. Take the time to think about this; don't confuse busyness and distraction with a lack of interest. Sacrifices you make today to accomplish your most important long-term goals ***will*** be worth it. Remember, the biggest determinant, humanly speaking, of your long-term financial progress and contentment is you.[34]

If you have identified giving, savings, investing, and debt-reduction conviction goals and are allocating money to them, congratulations! You have just created margin, and this will move you toward your goals. Now that you understand how to identify and label conviction giving and conviction margin, let's discuss your financial requirements.

---

[34] Hebrews 13:5 very simply says, "Be content with what you have." You have enough to be content because contentment is not dependent on how much you have. Paul wrote in Philippians 4:11-13, ". . . I have learned in whatever situation I am to be content . . ."

Requirements

Once you have identified how your convictions will dictate progress towards your most important goals, you should focus next on important responsibilities, or requirements, that you face. To be a faithful and prudent steward, what must you make sure to do? Certainly, a basic level of food, clothing, and shelter is a requirement – but I don't include them here; these will be discussed later as lifestyle *desires*.

There are several expenses that are not optional for a responsible steward to address. These include taxes, debt, and insurance. After all, your payroll and income taxes and minimum debt payments are contractual obligations. Every household should also make it a priority to consider, evaluate, and obtain adequate health insurance as well as life and disability insurance.[35]

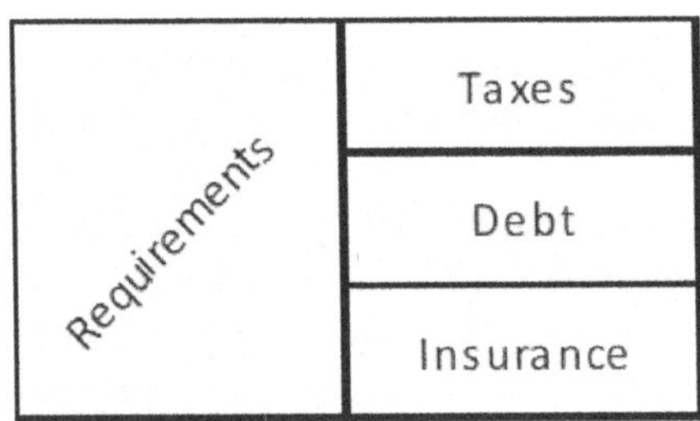

It is not necessarily a requirement that everyone pays for all these items all the time, but they must be evaluated. Choosing to go without appropriate insurance coverage may create adverse financial consequences down the road, so you need to own the decision to go without.

Taxes - Payroll and Income Taxes

The thought of paying your payroll and income taxes seems straightforward enough. In fact, for most people this is a non-factor. Taxes are withheld from paychecks and most people give

[35] I have never been compensated to sell any insurance products. My sole motivation in 'requiring' you to consider these insurance coverages is for you to make good stewardship choices.

little thought to these taxes consuming part of their available income.

At present, payroll taxes are currently 7.65% of a wage earner's gross pay, and these are deducted from your paycheck. Income taxes for federal (and most states) are in addition to the payroll taxes. The amount of income taxes you pay is based on several factors. The biggest factors at the current time include your gross income, marital status, and the number of children under age 16 in your home.

For traditional employees, federal and state income taxes are withheld from each paycheck.[36] Each spring you file a tax return with the federal government (and your state, if necessary) to compare how much income tax you should have paid during the year and how much you actually paid. If you paid more in income taxes throughout the year than proved necessary, you get a tax refund. If you did not pay enough during the year, you owe taxes when you file your return.

For good planning purposes, strive to have your tax withholdings on your paycheck match your expected tax liability for the year. This will take some math on your part but would allow you to anticipate filing a tax return in the spring that creates a $0 tax refund and $0 tax liability. Over the years as you get a good handle on your tax situation and develop a method to estimate your taxes accurately,[37] you may choose to set your withholdings to create a small refund (or liability).

---

[36] You can change how much income tax is withheld each pay period by changing your payroll setting with your employer.

[37] You may also ask your tax preparer, if you use one, to help you estimate the necessary withholdings. Be certain to anticipate how your income or tax-deductible expenses may change from one year to the next. Tax preparation only looks at events of the past – estimating this year's taxes requires you to anticipate how this year will be different.

Debt

If you have debt, you have made prior commitments that require regular payments. Generally, this means you have begun using (or have consumed) something before you have paid for it. For the purchase of some things, the use of debt may seem inevitable. In other cases, debt arises because you lack the patience to wait to buy something until you can pay using your current income or accumulated savings.

We are talking about credit cards, auto loans, student loans, 90-day same as cash loans for a fridge or sofa, mortgage debt, etc. that require recurring payments. It is prudent to also include rent payments (for a house or apartment) as a debt payment. This is helpful because you will either continue to pay the rent for housing indefinitely or you will replace the rent payment with a mortgage payment one day.

Finally, if you have a mortgage on your home, your mortgage payment may have multiple elements to it. It is quite possible that your one monthly mortgage payment includes principal and interest, escrow for property taxes and homeowner's insurance, and even possibly private mortgage insurance.

Calculating the minimum monthly debt payments is fairly easy. The required payments, for planning purposes, only count the minimum required payments for each debt. Any extra you choose to pay should be considered either a conviction for debt reduction or a use of margin.

Mortgage Warning...

There is a temptation to consider your mortgage as an eternal payment. It may seem so when you sign mortgage documents and you consider a payment schedule that often begins with 360 months of payments, but you must remember that you will eliminate the debt one day.

Don't live through your twenties, thirties, and forties assuming your mortgage payment is a foregone conclusion. If you do, you will probably refinance your debt a few times – each time on a new thirty-year amortization – and then becoming debt-free one day will require a massive downsizing in the value of your home. This will prove to be difficult.

Additionally, eliminating your mortgage debt while still working will provide you with a number of years to generate a significant amount of margin to better prepare for retirement. This may also facilitate a nicer retirement, an earlier retirement, more giving in retirement (charitable or family), a transition to a lower-paying job as a step towards retirement, or any number of other attractive opportunities.

Insurance - Health, Life, and Disability

You also have a significant responsibility, or requirement, to make sure that you address health insurance, as well as life and disability insurance.

Health Insurance

You must obtain health insurance. You may pursue coverage through your employer, a high deductible plan, an individual health care policy (when coverage is not available through an employer), or even a "Health Care Sharing" alternative. Regardless of which option you choose, it is important to provide adequate health insurance to make healthcare more accessible and to guard against medically induced financial calamities.

Coverage through an employer policy is generally preferred because employers typically heavily subsidize the monthly cost for the employee and the monthly premiums are usually paid on a pre-tax basis.

Lower-cost, higher deductible plans essentially turn coverage into a catastrophic health insurance plan. With these plans, you must include in your monthly budget the necessary monthly premiums and a monthly estimate for out-of-pocket costs.

Some health insurance alternatives called "Health Care Sharing" ministries or co-operatives may also be considered. These can be alternatives to traditional health insurance, but many come with enrollment requirements and may exclude coverage for certain pre-existing conditions. Beware of choosing this just because the monthly premium is lower. Research these arrangements carefully.

Long-term Disability

Long-term disability ("LTD") is important because this coverage can help replace your income should you be unable to work due to health reasons.[38]

LTD policies usually help replace lost income after you have been out of work for either 90 or 180 days. If triggered, the LTD policy will pay a monthly benefit until a typical retirement age like 65 or 67. Make sure to clarify the specifics, such as what constitutes a disability, and who decides if you meet these criteria. It is important to understand these definitions.

LTD can be expensive. As you can see, this type of policy may be required to pay benefits for a very long time. If a 26-year-old becomes disabled, the policy might pay you a monthly benefit for forty years.

Many larger employers provide employees with LTD policies that cover 60% of their income at no charge. This is a great benefit. If you have this coverage and become disabled, the policy will pay you 60% of your gross income until retirement or until you are no longer disabled. LTD proceeds from an employer-provided plan would be 100% taxable income.

---

[38] You should know there is also something called short-term disability insurance. I would suggest you not buy *short-term* disability because it generally only covers certain work disruptions that last less than 90 days. A good emergency fund can cover any work interruptions that are this short in duration.

If your employer provides LTD up to 60% of your gross income, you may consider supplementing this employer-provided coverage with an individually purchased "supplemental" LTD policy as your income rises. Generally, insurance companies will allow you to buy LTD policies that protect, in aggregate, up to 70% or 75% of your total gross earnings. Benefits paid from a supplemental LTD policy would be tax-free to the recipient.

Life Insurance

If you have any dependents who rely on you and your income, it is extremely important to purchase an appropriate amount of life insurance protection. Consider buying life insurance that may help replace your lost income in the event of your death.

If you are under 45 years old and have a net worth of under $2,000,000, you most likely should buy term-life insurance and not consider any other type of life insurance.[39]

Why is life insurance coverage so important? Consider what your dependents would do without you (and your income). If others are depending on your income and it is gone, how will they manage?

As a general rule, you may want to purchase a life insurance policy that provides a death benefit equal to ten times your salary. So, if you earn $60,000 a year, a term life insurance policy that has a $600,000 death benefit may be appropriate for you.

Many factors will determine if this death benefit amount is too high or too low for the dependents you leave behind. If married,

---

[39] In most cases, term life insurance is the best fit – even though it pays very little in commission to insurance salespeople. I regularly run into people who have bought permanent life insurance thinking they appropriately addressed their life insurance needs. Instead, in my opinion, they got too little coverage for way too much premium, and, despite their confidence and a large monthly payment, they did not protect what they set out to do. Term insurance is generally best for life insurance buyers - but not all.

does the surviving spouse work? Would your spouse continue earning at the same rate if you died? Do you have children? Do you have debts? What will your spouse do for housing? Do you want him to be forced to sell and move shortly after your death? Do you want your spouse to feel pressure to immediately increase earned income?

As you try to determine how much life insurance to buy, it may be best for you to identify a financial planner who can help you quantify your life insurance needs. It may not be best to rely on the counsel of a life insurance salesperson since they may lack objectivity.

One of the biggest financial mistakes you can make is to ignore purchasing appropriate life and LTD insurance policies. If you are earning money and others are depending on you (and your income), responsibly purchasing insurance is the primary way you can protect them.

If you died without providing for those who are depending on you, you would be revealing that your plan was to have your dependents completely change their lifestyle to cope. Or, perhaps, you were simply counting on others to step in to provide for your dependents. While there is certainly a place for the benevolence of others – families, friends, and a faith community – is it right for you to bypass taking prudent steps to provide for your family when you have the means to do so? Should you rely on others to make sacrifices to provide for your dependents when you could have but chose not to?

Lifestyle Desires

So far, in your cash flow, you have considered your income, your convictions, and your requirements. After you identify your conviction giving and margin and meet your requirements for taxes, debt, and insurance, you then have great freedom to spend all the leftover income on lifestyle needs and desires. Even if you spend all of this cash flow on current needs, you will still have created some margin because you directed income towards goals as a conviction.

Components of Lifestyle Spending

How do you begin tackling the project of fitting lifestyle spending into this number? Start by considering the spending items that are non-negotiable – or 'kind of' locked in.[40] These are spending items that are not discretionary such as utilities, a basic food budget, car insurance, basic transportation costs, etc.

You will then gravitate into areas that are more discretionary and, honestly, more fun. These may include travel, vacation, entertainment, eating out, weddings, and so on. These expenses can easily cause overspending because they are the more fun spending categories and can often appear non-negotiable.

Next, consider periodic expenses. Periodic expenses do not occur monthly like a power bill. Some periodic expenses are planned (like a vacation) and others are unplanned (like car repairs). They occur occasionally. Common examples include car maintenance and repairs, home repairs, holiday spending, summer vacation, etc. Often these expenses are unavoidable (i.e., once the car breaks down), and can be problematic because they are unknown in both the exact cost and timing. This often makes these items budget-killers.[41]

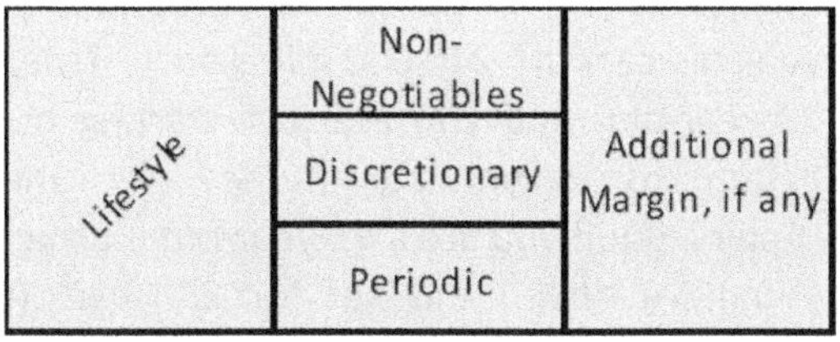

<table>
<tr><td rowspan="3">Lifestyle</td><td>Non-Negotiables</td><td rowspan="3">Additional Margin, if any</td></tr>
<tr><td>Discretionary</td></tr>
<tr><td>Periodic</td></tr>
</table>

---

[40] These are only 'kind-of' locked in because you could, if driven by circumstances or '1-mile-a-day' goals, reduce or eliminate these expenses by making major lifestyle changes. Moving to lower-cost housing is probably the easiest example of this. Since you may be reluctant to be this drastic, these expenses are 'kind-of' locked in.

[41] See Appendix 1 for some practical tips on how to plan and prepare for them.

Creating margin by fitting all your other expenses in the amount available can allow you to accelerate progress on these 'Eat-at-5-PM' goals. What you may find – and this will likely occur at every income level – is that you will be able to identify lifestyle desires that can't be squeezed into the available cash after convictions and requirements. This can create pressure or tension to reduce the money you committed to areas of conviction or shirk areas of responsibility. Spending too much requires you to spend down your existing cash balances, take on debt, or make difficult choices to cut other areas of your budget to make things work.

Commonly, people address a projected shortfall by neglecting the periodic and non-recurring budget line. They hold on and hope nothing bad happens. When the repair hits or the holidays arrive, they rationalize, "We had to fix the car, so we put it on the credit card," or "Of course, we weren't going to go without Christmas for the kids, so we charged $800 for presents."

Worse yet, people often play the victim because the expenses can be unpredictable. "I had to get the transmission fixed for $2,000. I had no choice. Unfortunately, I had to put all this on my credit card."

I get it. It happens. But did you build a budget for car maintenance and repairs that recognized you were driving a 16-year-old car with 240,000 miles on it? True, if this is your car as a 23-year-old, and you are just starting out, you will not have begun to accumulate money for these predictable car repairs. But if you are a 47-year-old making $120,000 a year, and you have driven this car for 23 years (Good for you!), you probably should have made some progress toward preparing for this repair. This would have been, at some point, a great candidate for a conviction savings goal.

So, if you are driving an older car, you must have a budget line item for car repair[42] and you can hope you never need it. If this is

---

[42] Everyone with a car needs a car maintenance budget item. Two oil

the case, the money is accumulating and can be used in the future for an eventual car repair or a future car purchase. If you own a home, you need a line item for home repair. Hot water heaters, HVAC systems, ceiling fans, disposals, washing machines, dishwashers, etc. will all eventually require some repair or replacement cost. Impossible to predict the amount and timing? Yes. Is the unpredictability reason enough to not set aside some money to address the inevitable? Of course not.

People who get tripped up by these periodic expenses are not bad people. Failing to prepare for them is not a moral failure. But many times, people don't recognize the relationship between the failure to prepare and the eventual debt that resulted. *Your goal is to make these oversights few and far between (and for small dollars) by acknowledging that these events will occur and demonstrating a willingness to adjust other lifestyle spending areas to accommodate them.*

> If you allow your spending to exceed your available cash this year, what will compel you to limit your spending to what is available next year?

Acknowledge it, decide on it, and do something about it.[43] Limit self-inflicted problems.

What if the Lifestyle Spending Doesn't Fit?

If you are unable to limit your spending to the amount available after the convictions and requirements, you will either be forced to reduce your conviction-use of money, shirk financial requirements, reduce lifestyle spending, borrow money, or pull

---

changes a year and tires every five years will create the need for a monthly savings amount.

[43] Have I told you the riddle about the frogs on the log?

from your existing cash balances. Each of these is problematic and unsustainable. Borrowing money will increase your debt payments and therefore increase your future spending on requirements – which will make creating margin even harder. You simply can't pull from your cash balances forever. If you allow your spending to exceed your available cash this year, *what will compel you to limit your spending to what is available in the future*?

At some point, you must limit lifestyle spending decisions to match your available income. Y*ou want* your income, convictions, and requirements to dictate your lifestyle spending. Don't reverse this. Don't let lifestyle spending and housing choices dictate how much money is available for everything else.

To build wealth you must create margin and do so repeatedly.

Creating More Margin

If you want to create additional margin beyond the conviction margin you have prioritized, you need to spend less than the maximum available on lifestyle spending. In other words, you have made '1-mile-a-day' progress by committing some income to your convictions. You can make progress on the 'Eat-at-5-PM' goals by limiting lifestyle spending to create additional margin.

Having a plan to create additional margin is a good idea. This can allow you to pay for other expenses that may arise and exceed your budget for whatever reason. If you can sustain the creation of monthly margin over a period of time, you can redirect the margin to make faster progress toward your goals.

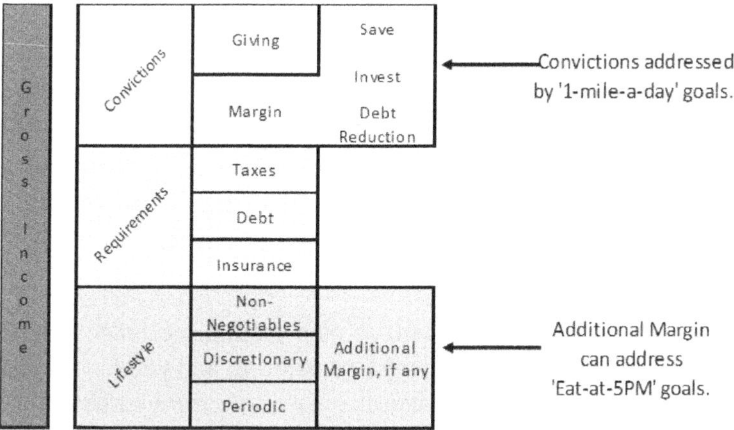

This takes maturity which most people gain through experience. Why wait? The sooner you learn this, the better.[44]

A typical 26-year-old may say, "It will be easier to create margin when I am older and my income is higher."

A typical 56-year-old probably despairs, "If I had only saved more money when I was 26 and didn't have the responsibilities I have now - the mortgage, the kids, the house, the car. If I only knew then what I know now."

The ability to create margin can allow you to be better prepared for your goals. Picture all the grandchildren helping Grammy prepare dinner.[45] This help would provide Grammy more margin which may allow her to serve dinner at 5 PM.

You may also have some important goals that aren't truly convictions, but you still want to meet them. That is the power of margin creation – you can use it to make that progress.

---

[44] Proverbs 4:1 commends young people for learning from instruction from older people. "Hear, O sons, a father's instruction, and be attentive, that you may gain insight..."

[45] To be fair, Grammy's son-in-law could also pitch in, I guess.

Pulling It All Together

It is one thing to identify your goals and plot out your cash flow spending, but it is another thing to make everything fall into place. The definitions seem straightforward, and theoretically, the labeling and prioritizing of your budget items seem neat and tidy. Identifying convictions about long-term goals seems almost freeing.

As if in a dream, imagine you've paid off the mortgage on the house, the white picket fence stays painted, and you have great neighbors. Unexpected expenses only arise after you have pre-funded them in a savings account[46] and you magically withhold the exact amount of tax money on your paystubs. Your employer subsidizes your health insurance, matches your 401k and your annual pay increases always exceed inflation. Your 2.3 children have perfect teeth (no braces for them!), everyone is satisfied with the (low) grocery budget, no one ever wants to eat out, and you have complete and utter marital harmony for every conceivable financial decision.

Or not.

Adopting common language and definitions around your cash flow can make the process easier. Clarifying and even quantifying[47] financial goals help define convictions. Giving sacrificially can provide you joy by meeting the needs of others and help you cultivate contentment over the long term.

But it's not that simple. Matthew Broderick, as the fictional Ferris Bueller, once said, "Life comes at you fast." Feared heavyweight boxing champion Mike Tyson once reportedly said, "Everyone has a plan until they get punched in the face."

Life does come at you fast and (hopefully) all your 'punches in the face' are figurative. Even with good planning and clearly defined

---

[46] This makes them almost seem like *expected* expenses.

[47] And re-clarifying and re-quantifying on a regular basis!

goals, the *implementation* of a good cash flow framework is always more difficult than its creation. Trying to spread your income across convictions, requirements, and lifestyle desires has two major challenges:

1. Make it work on paper.

2. Make it work in real life.

Can you Make it Work on Paper?

Organizing convictions, requirements, and lifestyle needs and desires into your income comes with obvious challenges. Your conviction goals may be unrealistic at first. Also, expenses - especially periodic expenses - can be unpredictable.

Goals may be Unrealistic

It is possible you have identified some convictions that are too costly. For example, you may have said your most compelling financial convictions are to pay for three kids to go to a private college, you want to be debt-free by age 55 and you want to retire at 60 so you can volunteer 30 hours a week. If your current salary at age 26 is $180,000, you can probably make great progress on each of these goals starting right now. Perhaps you can devote monthly investment contributions to each of these objectives that put you on a linear trajectory[48] to achieve all of them. But if your income is more modest, no matter how sincere your goals and how spartan your lifestyle, you may simply not be able to devote the required amount of money to these goals and have enough left over for food and shelter.

---

[48] What is linear trajectory? Making linear progress to meet a long-term goal would anticipate you would save the same amount each month towards a goal; saving $30 each month will allow you to save $360 in one year. Non-linear ways to save would include saving $360 in a year by saving $20 a month for six months and then $40 in the next six months. You might pay down debt by paying $100 extra this year and $200 extra next year, etc.

The truth is that making linear progress on your most important long-term goals may be unrealistic at the start. If you can't invest $200 monthly in a college savings account right now, you may need to start with $75 a month. This smaller monthly investment may serve as a reminder (and encouragement, I hope) that you are contributing what you can for now and that your convictions should prompt you to increase the monthly savings as your income rises or as other goals are achieved.

If you are not able to fit all your conviction margin into your current cash flow, you will simply have to start with a smaller conviction margin. This is not defeat. Your financial life is not over. Begin with what you are able and strive to make it a priority to limit future spending so you can direct more future income to your '1-mile-a-day' goals. Making some progress is better than making none.[49]

Expenses are Unpredictable

Expenses can be very unpredictable. You simply cannot control all the circumstances you will encounter. Some future expenses are disguised as opportunities[50] and some are simply lurking in the background waiting to surprise you.

Get married? Move? Change jobs? Have a baby? Be asked to be a bridesmaid? You will stumble on seemingly wonderful opportunities, be confronted with potentially life-altering decisions, and simply run into the unexpected. "Life comes at you fast!" Imagine hearing one of these:

- My uncle is offering us his car for a great price, but we have to decide this week.
- What? Twins? Are you sure?
- The boss gave me a 15% raise to be a shift manager but wants me to move to a plant 85 miles away.

---

[49] Is anything wrong with an initial goal to run ½ mile a day? You can then later build up to 1 mile-a-day one day, right?

[50] Or are they opportunities disguised as expenses?

- The doctor said the test results weren't great, and I need to go in next week to learn more.
- Junior may have a learning disability. They are recommending more after-school tutoring.
- Mom and Dad just called. They want to come for 5 days next month.
- The ultrasound revealed some irregularities. This is a high-risk pregnancy and there may be abnormalities. We will learn more next week.
- My aunt just gave me a $50 gift card for my birthday. Is our family gifting budget high enough?[51]

In real life, an ideal cash flow plan can be turned upside down very quickly. Your task, over time, is to prevent these unexpected events from totally derailing the financial progress that helps you reach your '1-mile-a-day' goals. These events certainly influence your goals, but they don't always have to redefine them.

If you find yourself repeatedly running into interruptions that prevent progress, you may not really have conviction goals after all. Honestly assess this as you see how progress is made or interrupted for a season. Picture me with a refill of tortilla chips, commenting on my desire to lose weight.

Periodic expenses are especially tricky. What are your desired (and affordable) options for vacations and holidays? How old are your cars? Will you spend money on preventive expenses for your teeth and your car? When you buy a home, you assume many upkeep and maintenance responsibilities that your former landlord used to cover like the water heater, kitchen appliances, washer and dryer, crawl space, HVAC, roof, chimney, siding, windows, etc.

You must build some room in your budget for items that only show up periodically - especially if they are unpredictable. You can find some good practical tips on how to prepare for these types of expenses in Appendix 1. Building a budget on paper that

[51] No. My birthday is in April – just two months before Father's Day.

ignores these periodic future expenses is like studying for a spelling test by studying only 60% of the available words. Your unpreparedness may not be revealed on the first test. Take enough tests, however, and you will miss a lot of words.[52]

So, on paper, if the math isn't working you may have to re-evaluate how much progress towards your long-term convictions is realistic *at this time*. Beware of making a budget on paper that ignores important periodic expenses. Be as thoughtful as you can to be prepared for realistic expenses that will come your way.

I want to provide a word of caution. When you identify a long-term goal as a conviction, it may certainly seem outlandish and unreasonable based on your circumstances today. It may be easy to explain away or justify why you can't do it now but be careful. You can always find reasons to spend more now and save less for later. Try to identify why you can't or won't create the conviction margin that fits with your long-term goals.

Re-evaluating the reasonableness of your long-term convictions will prompt you to stare hard at the tension between 'current lifestyle desires' and 'future lifestyle desires'. Do your long-term convictions call for you to reduce your lifestyle spending now? Do you place a higher value on the enjoyment today or the financial flexibility you can have in the future?

As you weigh these competing desires, try to frame up the actual choices you are making. For example, "We just cannot save enough for college to meet our number one conviction right now" might actually be better framed this way, "We can't afford to save for that college savings goal if we stay in this house. But we could save more for college if we choose to move to another house that is cheaper to own and maintain." Ask yourself, "Do

---

[52] Warren Buffet has a famous quote for having a portfolio that is too risky, "You never know who is swimming naked until the tide goes out." That sentiment, but not the imagery, fits here. You can get away with not being prepared for home and car maintenance for a while. Eventually, you will be found out!

we really value college savings more than our current housing situation? If we spent less on housing, could we make more progress toward college savings? Which is more important to us right now?"[53]

So, you have wrestled with your spending plan on paper. Maybe it looks exactly like you want. Maybe you think you have a reasonable categorization that includes your convictions (even if not fully funded at the outset), requirements, and a reasonable current lifestyle budget. Great!

Can you Make it Work in Real Life?

Organizing your convictions, requirements, and lifestyle desires takes time and can be hard. Implementation can be just as difficult.

If your income rises from $55,000 to $85,000 over a few years and you still cannot muster up any money for a short or long-term conviction goal, you probably don't have an 'unexpected expense' problem; you may have a contentment problem, an honesty problem, or both.

Be honest with yourself: Do you really want to save money for the next car, so you won't take on so much debt? Do you really want your long-term plan to be "We will figure it out"? Do you wonder how people in a similar life stage who make $10,000 less than you can possibly survive?[54] Are you willing to admit that you

---

[53] These types of questions are really designed for you to determine what you value more. You may value the experience of being in a nicer housing situation. That's fine - that won't disappoint anyone else. You don't need to save for college to satisfy anyone else. You are responsible for how you spend your money.

[54] Generally, it is not a great idea to compare yourself to others. Most of the 'others' are borrowing money and living on 105 to 110 percent of their income - that is hard to keep up with! But when you think you can't live without something or some service, realize that others who make less than you are managing to make it without that particular item or service.

value *all* your current spending more than making any progress on *any* of your long-term goals?

If you are struggling to make any progress, I suggest you reexamine your goals. What is truly most important to you? What things are worthy of dictating other spending levels? Have you accurately captured your short-term and long-term goals?

Creating a spending plan on paper is hard. Even if done right with some good forward-thinking, it may seem impossible. Working at it – using it as a tool to really define what is most important to you - is valuable. Implementing the plan and constantly revising it is work. It is work that you will be glad you did now. Your 55-year-old self will be more glad that you prioritized your current cash flow to accommodate longer-term goals.

Pulling It All Together – The Numbers

Let's review the cash flow for a combined gross income of exactly $100,000 and see how this may all fit together.

Income

	Total
Gross Pay	100,000
Payroll tax FICA	7,650
Federal Income Tax	7,491
State Income Tax	3,306
401k Pre-tax	6,000
HI Pre-tax	2,400
Net pay	73,153

Conviction Giving and Conviction Margin

We will assume you want to give 10% of your gross income away.[55] This will use $10,000 of your annual income.

Let's assume you desire to buy a $225,000 house in the coming years with a $22,500 down payment. You want to devote enough cash flow to a conviction savings goal to build your current $5,000 cash balance to $22,500 in two years. At a minimum, this will require saving $17,500 over two years – that's $8,750 annually or about $729 a month.

To maximize your employer match on your retirement account, you are investing $6,000 into retirement accounts.

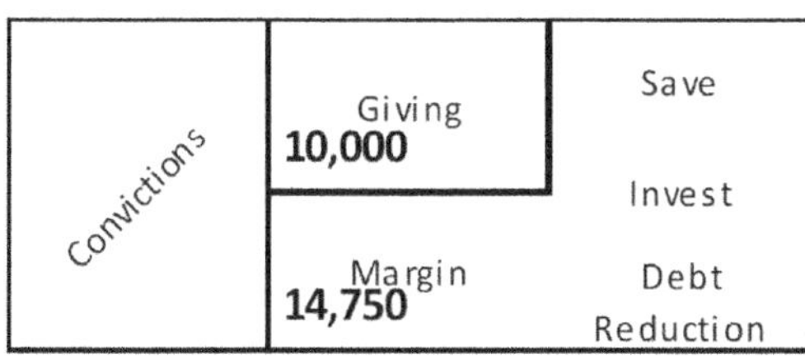

Requirements

You have set payroll deductions at a rate that you believe will cover your income and payroll taxes. These three tax totals from your pay stub equal $18,447 annually.

Currently, you have no debt, but you currently rent an apartment that costs $1,600 per month, or $19,200 over the course of a year.[56] You really wanted to rent a nicer place, one in a trendier

---

[55] A commitment like this simply requires faith. You can see that other savings and investing goals and lifestyle desires could use a boost with more available cash – but committing money to spiritual or philanthropic efforts does come at a financial cost. The faith aspect says, "I believe this is best for me and others even when I can see tangible ways not giving will benefit me." You can easily see how giving like this becomes sacrificial.

[56] For reference, a mortgage on a $225,000 house with 10% down at an annual interest rate of 6%, might look like this with about $6,000

part of town that resembled your childhood neighborhood. Instead, you chose a less expensive apartment because you wanted to be able to buy a house sooner.

You also have purchased health insurance through, and subsidized by, your employer. These premiums are paid on your paystub and total $2,400.

Currently, your employer provides disability coverage for 60% of your gross income at no cost to you, and you believe this coverage is sufficient. As your income rises, you know this should be reevaluated.

At present, since you have no children and no debt, you believe life insurance is not required. However, since you anticipate taking on mortgage debt in a few years and you are healthy, you have gone ahead and purchased two small life insurance policies. You know that you will need more should you have children, but for now, you have purchased two policies: A 30-year level term policy for one of you comes with a $500,000 death benefit and a similar policy on a spouse with a death benefit of $250,000 comes with annual premiums of $336 and $180 for a total of $516. When combined with your health insurance costs, the total insurance cost for the year is $2,916.

Requirements		
	18,447	Taxes
	19,200	Debt
	2,916	Insurance

Now that convictions and requirements are identified, you can build a line-by-line budget for all remaining expenses. You must

---

payable in closing costs: Principal and Interest payment of $1,214 and escrow estimates of $150/monthly for property taxes, $80 for home insurance and $60 for PMI insurance. The total resulting mortgage payment is $1,504.

determine how much of your gross income is left for all other expenses.

How Much is Available for Lifestyle Spending?

Now, your job is to build a budget to address all other spending needs and desires that total up to no more than $34,687. Keep in mind, you do not need to use any of this $34,687 for your 10% giving, your conviction margin, your taxes, rent, health insurance, or life or disability insurance. These expenses are already covered with your convictions and requirements.

Gross Income			
	Convictions	Giving 10,000	Save Invest Debt Reduction
		Margin 14,750	
	Requirements	18,447 Taxes	
		19,200 Debt	
		2,916 Insurance	
	Available 34,687 Lifestyle	Non-Negotiables	Additional Margin, if any
		Discretionary	
		Periodic	

You then want to start your list of lifestyle expenses that are, based on current circumstances, not really negotiable. These will include such items as basic food costs, basic transportation costs (insurance and gas), and basic utilities.

The word 'basic' is used to highlight the fact that you are starting with necessary food costs first – you are not starting with the 'this is all the extravagant items from a grocery store that I can ever want' list. You are starting with the 'I have some convictions and requirements that are so important that they compel me to limit my spending in other areas if necessary' list for food items. Do you see the difference?

Therefore, start with the basics – maybe the minimum grocery budget you can realistically get by with. You can easily find lists of common household expenses to include in your budget.

You will work through other expenses that start to include more discretionary and fun items like eating out and traveling.[57] Your background and personal experience may really shape your thinking here and will probably create challenges and advantages. If you are married, these positives and negatives may be amplified or neutralized, or they may be a source of significant tension.

Finally, include budget categories for periodic expenses to address repairs and maintenance of your cars and housing. Include gifts, travel, holiday spending, weddings, etc. Include a monthly total to be set aside for these items - even if you expect to go a few months with no spending for any of these items.

One Challenge

One significant challenge you may encounter is the unspoken expectation that you continue the lifestyle spending that you were accustomed to while you lived at home just a few years ago. Some of these spending habits may feel ingrained as 'normal' or even 'necessary' because you enjoyed these from ages 14 to 22 – your entire teenage and adult life.

You are used to eating out at a certain frequency and at certain restaurants. You are also accustomed to certain vacation experiences, entertainment packages, cell phone replacement

---

[57] Crown Financial Ministries website has some great resources for this online, but you can also find a slew of lists just about anywhere.

cycles, clothing purchases, etc. You may have enjoyed your family paying for them (perhaps even quite responsibly) because your parents have worked and saved and are operating their household budget on an income that is significantly higher than yours because, by this time, *they have been working for 25 or 30 years longer than you!* Recognize this danger and be mindful of default spending choices that you may not be prepared for yet.

Results

Once you add up your list of budgeted lifestyle expenses you will see either margin or a deficit. (Unless the budget number matches the income amount exactly.)

If you are at a deficit, you may have to revisit some of your convictions. Maybe saving enough for your desired down payment in two years is too unrealistic. That's possible. Maybe you must revisit some of your requirements. Perhaps you aren't able to buy the life insurance coverage 'early' and you should wait on this purchase until you incur mortgage debt or have children. Another possible solution is to revisit some of your lifestyle spending categories.

If it appears you have additional margin, great! You may simply transfer this amount each month to your savings account and expect to see your savings grow each month. Perhaps you will need this money if you end up going over budget during the year, or perhaps at the end of the year you will have the confidence to transfer the cash into some other account.

So why does the popsicle stick appear to be larger than an 870-foot-tall building? It is fairly simple. The popsicle stick appears to be taller because it is so close, and the building is so far away. I want you to imagine writing "Current Lifestyle Desires" on the popsicle stick and hanging a banner on the 60-story building that says, "Long-Term Goals."

Your desires and needs to spend today appear to be much more pressing because they are right in front of you – like the popsicle stick on top of Crowders Mountain. The long-term goals you may have for education, caring for an elderly parent, or your own retirement seem small and less important because they are so distant – you can't even read the banner on the building 30 miles away![58]

If you continued to hold the popsicle stick with your arm extended and walked from the mountain to Charlotte, you would get extremely tired, observe that the size of the popsicle stick never changed, notice the Charlotte skyline would appear to be getting larger with every half mile or so, and eventually see that the buildings were actually enormous.

So it is, as you get older. What appeared to be so large and important in your past oftentimes turns out to be relatively small.[59] What seemed so distant and unimportant before, now appears rather intimidating.

> What appeared to be so large and important in your past oftentimes turns out to be relatively small.

So many people get distracted and orient their priorities and spending around immediate needs while neglecting to set any money aside for the long term. They see the size of the popsicle stick and the immediacy of their daily wants and needs

---

[58] Seriously, how would you hang a banner on this building anyway?

[59] Have you ever helped a couple dispossess themselves of their lifetime accumulated 'stuff' when downsizing? Have you ever visited an estate sale? These scenes provide some perspective on what becomes of the once, shiny new purchases.

and find it difficult to appreciate the significance of future values and desires.

You've identified your '1-mile-a-day' and 'Eat-at-5-PM' goals. Now let these goals dictate spending choices to create margin. What exactly do you do with this margin? We will tackle that next.

Exhortation Four
SAVE AND INVEST YOUR MARGIN

While watching the 2021 NCAA Track and Field National Championship in Eugene, Oregon, you see Micah Williams, from the host Oregon Ducks track team, run 100 meters in an amazing time of 10.11 seconds. In a separate race, you watch Micah's teammate, Cole Hocker, run 100 meters in 14.35 seconds.

Was Micah or Cole faster? Which runner do you think would win in a head-to-head race?

△ △ △ △ △ △

Procrastination. I've waited this long to bring it up and I just couldn't wait any longer.

A fishing trip with a local guide at the nearest lake next month is better than an extravagant fishing trip with a world-famous guide on the best lake that never takes place. Sometimes people create grand plans wanting to make an experience perfect, but then they sadly never get around to it. To quote from the introduction of this book, "...pretty good can be the enemy of completed."

I am not suggesting you settle or compromise when you don't have to, but getting started investing right now with a good plan will pay more dividends for you than waiting until you think you have a perfect plan. Perfect plans rarely get implemented.[60]

In your cash flow, your margin has been created by establishing (and following through on) a conviction goal or by spending less than the income left over after the convictions, requirements and lifestyle spending, or both:

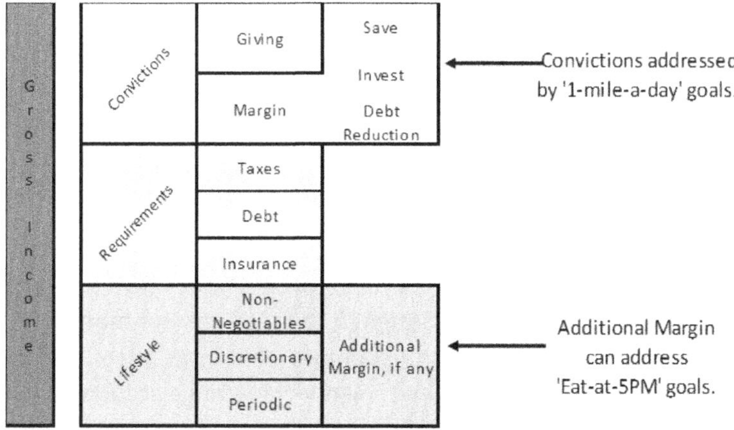

Your '1-mile-a-day' and 'Eat-at-5PM' goals have dictated these spending limits to create margin. You now need to save or invest this margin *today* to provide the best possible *future* outcome.

Investment Knowledge

Before we go any further, let's consider these key points on the limitations of our conversation on investing:

---

[60] The same sentiment can be crippling in other areas of life. "I don't want to get married now. I am just not ready yet." or "We'll try to start having kids when we are ready." This may be good, healthy prudence, but you may never feel truly 'ready' for marriage or kids. You can wait fifty years, and you will still not feel ready. Sometimes you have to just tackle the challenge and do the best you can. See Kevin DeYoung's *Just Do Something*.

1. This section on investing basics is not designed to qualify you for any wealth management certification or make you an attractive candidate for any financial advisor role.
2. When your investments exceed $50,000 in combined value, it makes sense to consult with a fee-only financial professional to develop a comprehensive long-term strategy and to define appropriate securities for each of your accounts.

With this in mind, let's examine several key aspects to know about investing.

The Difference Between Saving and Investing

For our purposes, the terms 'savings' and 'investments' are different.

You are building savings when you deposit money into a low-risk, low-return account that is designed to preserve your money and provide a very small return. Examples of savings accounts are FDIC-insured checking, savings, high-yield savings accounts, and Certificates of Deposit ("CDs"). Money market accounts are also commonly used as savings accounts.

The rates of return on typical savings accounts are almost always lower than inflation. Inflation is a measurement of the changes in the price of things. When prices are rising, the economy experiences inflation and stuff costs more. A savings account rate of return may be 3% per year. If the cost of college expenses is rising at 6% per year, your 3% savings return is not keeping up with inflation. As a result, savings accounts may be appropriate for some purposes, but not for all.

For our purposes, you are investing when you are buying securities that are designed, but not guaranteed, to provide higher rates of returns than the guaranteed rates available in common savings vehicles.

Investments inside accounts designed for retirement or education come with certain income tax advantages, but they also come with some limitations. You can also invest directly in non-retirement accounts that have virtually no limitations with dozens of online brokerages. There are so many different ways you can invest.

Diversification in Investing is Important

People who build extravagant amounts of wealth generally have very concentrated investment portfolios. People who build wealth more gradually and preserve it generally have a well-diversified portfolio.

Concentrating wealth can lead to extravagant wealth. To make an appearance on the Forbes 400 list of the world's wealthiest people, you have to start a company whose products or services become omnipresent globally. You must concentrate all your assets on the business and take an extraordinary risk. This rarely leads to fame and fortune; this type of concentrated risk more often leads to massive and permanent losses. Building and preserving wealth over a long period of time is most often accomplished through diversified investment portfolios that incorporate careful risk management.

When you invest with a diversified strategy, you invest a small amount of money in a large number of securities. By doing so, you virtually eliminate the likelihood of phenomenal investment gains, but you also virtually eliminate the possibility of catastrophic losses. If you are reading this book, chances are overwhelming that your best path to building sizable wealth is dependent on you creating margin over and over and investing your margin in a sensible, long-term strategy.[61]

---

[61] You may invest in any number of ways. Our discussion will gravitate toward traditional stock and bond investing. If you invest in properties, or start and grow a business, the principles we discuss will carry over to the investment choices you make - even if untraditional.

When you start investing, you generally start with a small dollar amount. While your investment balance is low, you may find it appealing to buy a single security rather than diversify more broadly. After all, buying one stock provides more excitement than a broadly diversified strategy. As your investment balances grow, it is prudent and wise to manage risk carefully. A prudent long-term investor will diversify a portfolio so that it is highly likely that their expected long-term return will be close to 'market averages' rather than attempt to catch lightning in a bottle and risk their assets to chase supercharged, and extremely unlikely, investment returns.

There is a Relationship Between Risk and Reward

An elementary understanding of the relationship between the risk of an investment and its expected return is necessary to help you invest properly. It would be great if you could make an investment that has a high expected return and a low amount of risk. In short, ***these do not exist***. If you think you have found an investment that has a high return and very little risk, you do not understand all the risks involved.

When you want a low-risk investment, you have to accept the expectation of getting a small return. When you desire a higher investment return, you have to be willing to accept more risk. It's just that simple. An important part of investing is having realistic expectations for your investment and structuring your investments based on the returns you are seeking and the risks you are comfortable taking.

You have to recognize that great returns are not available without taking a significant risk. Additionally, you do not want to take a high level of risk when the expected return is low. In investing terms, you want your investments to be efficient. As the risk of a particular investment goes up, you want the expected return to go up as well.

All material investments, even the safest, require risk. Some investments may provide guarantees ensuring no loss of principal, but other risks *are* still present.

For example, an FDIC-insured savings account has a guaranteed rate of return and a guaranteed return of principal. If inflation outpaces the rate of return, however, you will continue to lose purchasing power as long as you hold the money in this account. Therefore, you risk jeopardizing your current lifestyle spending even if your principal is guaranteed from loss. Similarly, investing in an ultra-conservative manner may guarantee you a smooth ride with no investment losses, but you may run a tremendous risk of running out of assets before you die.

Low-risk, low-return, safe investments will tend to provide a more stable return, but they will grow slowly. There is little chance of high returns in safe investments. Risk can manifest itself in several ways. The higher the risk of an investment, the greater the uncertainty that investment gains will materialize at all. While the desired returns may materialize over a longer period of time, the short-term returns you have to endure to achieve the desired long-term investment return may vary widely. This variability severely tests the patience of the most confident investor.

Risk and Time Horizon

The time horizon for an investment is the intended period of time between the initial investment and the ultimate withdrawal of the funds. As an investor, the time horizon for your investment is a major determinant of how aggressively or conservatively to invest. You can see how a boring, FDIC-insured savings account can be appropriate for a car purchase planned nine months in the future. You want the best return you can, but you don't want to put your car money at risk. If your car money is invested aggressively and it drops 4% in two weeks, the aggressive investment may not recover the 4% loss in time to buy the car.

So, as you build an investment portfolio it is imperative that you match your investment goals with the appropriate time horizon. This makes it easier to determine the kind of return that is reasonable and the amount of risk you can stomach and will make building an investment portfolio[62] much easier.

For emergency funds and for money set aside for major purchases in the near future, conservative strategies are best. If the primary purpose is preservation, and there is no tolerance for loss of principal, you may actually use a savings account rather than an investment account. In fact, this savings (which is not an investment) is crucial to building a good investment strategy. The presence of your emergency fund and major purchase savings accounts allows you to be more aggressive with the rest of your current investable assets and future margin.

For retirement money that will be used in forty years or more, you can stomach fluctuations in value over the short term *as long as* you have confidence your investments will recover over the long haul. This allows you to invest more aggressively.

Investing in college for a 2-year-old also calls for a longer time horizon and allows for a fairly high appetite for risk. While you would like your account to go up 9% every year, you can probably live with some variability in investment returns, as long as you remain confident that your long-term strategy is sound. This same patience is especially suitable for retirement investing, but your tolerance for risk - whether it is the risk of loss or just enduring the variability of returns - should be much lower for an investment goal as it gets closer.

You can rightly assume that there is a middle ground for investments with a time horizon between two and forty years. If you want to accumulate money for a house down payment that is 3 to 5 years away, you may want to invest more aggressively than in an FDIC-insured savings account. You certainly would not

---

[62] An investment portfolio is just a collection of individual securities which may be in one or more accounts.

want to take the same risk as you do in a retirement account. In this case, you want to build a moderate strategy that has a good chance of outperforming the FDIC-insured savings account, while carefully limiting the potential losses.

Common Types of Accounts

There are many types of investment accounts serving a variety of purposes. Some of the more common ones are described below, beginning with the accounts that have the longest investment time horizon.

Retirement Investing

Some investment accounts are specifically set up to provide for retirement investing. These accounts generally provide current or future tax incentives related to contributions, earnings, or withdrawals. Tax-favored retirement accounts can be established through an employer-provided plan like a 401(k) or a 403(b),[63] or set up by an individual using an IRA or a Roth IRA.[64]

Some contributions to employer-provided plans allow you to get matching contributions. If offered by your employer, this powerful incentive should create a '1-mile-a-day' goal for you to contribute at least enough to maximize any possible company match.

Employer-provided retirement plans have these characteristics:

- Contributions can be 'traditional' or 'Roth'. The type of contribution you designate determines which tax benefits you want to enjoy. This is an important decision, but there is not a universal best choice.

---

[63] Non-profit corporations use 403(b) accounts, while for-profit companies use 401(k) accounts. These accounts are named for the section of the tax code that established them - impress your friends with that knowledge.

[64] An IRA is an abbreviation for Individual Retirement Account. They got this one right!

- Investment choices inside these plans are usually limited, but this list should provide opportunities to build an aggressive portfolio.
- Employer-provided plans have annual contribution limits and some strict withdrawal rules that can become quite complicated. The limited access to these funds is a major trade-off that you must endure to take advantage of the tax benefits these plans offer.

If you are not employed, or your employer does not offer a retirement plan, you may be able to enjoy some of the tax benefits available to employer-provided plan contributions and investments by opening and contributing to individual retirement accounts. These are called IRAs and Roth IRAs. In some cases, you may be able to contribute to these individual retirement accounts in addition to participating in an employer-provided plan.

Individual retirement accounts have these characteristics:

- Contributions to IRAs have complicated rules and limitations based on many factors including your earned income for the year, your age, your total contributions to any employer-provided plans available to you, and other factors.
- IRAs and Roth IRAs can be opened at dozens of large brokerages or at most banks, and the investment possibilities are virtually endless. You can invest in just about anything.

Lastly, when you leave an employer, you can 'roll over' your assets from the employer-provided plan to an IRA or a Roth IRA based on the nature of original contributions to the plan. As your assets grow in value, the flexibility to invest in an IRA or Roth IRA is a tremendous advantage over being stuck with the limited choices available in most employer-provided plans.[65]

Non-retirement Investing - General (Individual or Joint)

You can also invest in an account that is not considered a retirement account. In this type of account, you can buy essentially the same types of investment vehicles, but these accounts are simply taxed differently. Non-retirement accounts do not have any contribution or withdrawal limitations.

Non-retirement accounts can be owned by one person or owned jointly, meaning two people share ownership. These accounts are taxed to the owner based on the activity inside the account every year. The receipt of interest, dividends, and the sales of securities can create taxable gains or losses that affect your current year's tax return. If you recognize taxable gains inside your account during the year, you may have to pay more income tax. This isn't necessarily bad, but it may influence your investment choices. This is yet another reason a fee-only investment professional may be worthwhile as your asset values (and tax bracket) rise.

From a tax perspective, retirement accounts are better for you. Generally, you can only access retirement accounts at retirement age. As a result, the use of non-retirement funds may be a better fit for some goals - even with the potential for incurring taxes along the way.[66] The higher your tax rate and the

---

[65] It is amazing to me that many employer-provided retirement plans are designed so poorly. Over the years, I have seen some very large companies provide employees with a list of funds that only includes one bond fund or one international stock fund. Considering some of their older employees nearing retirement may have $2,000,000 in their accounts, companies should provide a broader list of choices to allow employees to diversify their portfolios.

[66] Tax laws - often meant to influence behavior - do encourage investors to own securities for a longer period of time. Generally, investors can

larger your investment balance, the greater emphasis you need to place on tax efficiency as you purchase and manage your non-retirement investment portfolio.

529 accounts - Education Investing

Five twenty-nine, or "529", investment accounts are the most common investment vehicle for investing for future post-high school educational expenses.[67] 529 accounts are established by individual states and come in several shapes and sizes. You can typically buy them directly from a state (no commissions paid) or you can buy the almost identical 529 investment options in an advisor-sold 529 that comes with some broker fees.

In a 529 account, you can invest money today and then later withdraw your contributions *and earnings* to pay for qualifying education expenses without paying tax on the investment earnings. If you start when a child is young enough, it is possible to get over twenty years of investment growth without paying income tax on the gains. The longer the money is invested, the larger the potential to enjoy tax-free growth. Again, there are many rules and restrictions, but using a 529 plan to save for college expenses can be a powerful investment tool.

Like retirement accounts, investments in 529 accounts have restrictions on the timing and taxation of future withdrawals. Each state 529 plan has a list of investments - like a company 401k fund lineup - to choose from. These fund lineups are typically not extensive, but they do provide you with an array of choices ranging from conservative to aggressive. The

---

pay lower 'capital gains' tax rates on the sales of securities that are sold more than 1 year after purchase.

[67] A few years ago, the 529 rules were changed to allow up to $10,000 of annual withdrawals to pay for qualifying educational expenses paid for before college - such as private school expenses. Remember, the maximum advantage of the 529 is to enjoy gains for the longest period of time - since that can allow for more gains to be tax-free.

tremendous opportunity for tax-free growth makes these very appealing tools for savings for future college goals.

Common Types of Securities

Opening an investment account, whether it be for retirement, education or a non-retirement investment is not enough. Once you open and fund the account with an initial contribution (and hopefully set up recurring transfers into the account), you still have to invest the money by buying a security.

Stocks and bonds are the two most common investment 'ingredients'. What follows is a brief, high-level description of stocks and bonds.

Right now, in the United States, there are over 5,000 publicly traded American companies that have stock outstanding. When you buy a stock, you become an owner of that company. As you might imagine, there are many different types of companies; this allows you to buy stocks with a variety of characteristics. Some are steady and can provide more consistent returns. Some companies are trying to grow very aggressively even at the risk of complete failure.

An investor can also buy stock in companies that are headquartered in foreign countries. The political, economic, currency, and even cultural differences in overseas markets can provide an expanded set of investment opportunities in foreign stocks.

Bonds are another common form of investment. Bonds are often called 'fixed income securities', and they represent the debt of a company. If you buy a bond, you are actually loaning money to a company at the terms set up by the company.[68] There are

---

[68] The Company that creates the bond chooses the terms - you simply decide whether to loan them the money ("buy the bond") or not. Federal, state, and local government agencies also borrow money by selling bonds.

actually a greater variety of bonds available to invest in than there are stocks.

Each bond issued by a company or governmental entity has characteristics like the interest rate it will pay and the duration of the bond. While you might think the higher-interest rate is good for the investor, high-interest costs may make it harder for the company to stay in business. As a bond investor, you need the company to stay in business so that it can repay the bond at maturity.[69] Needless to say, bonds can be complicated.

Stocks tend to be more aggressive, and bonds tend to be more conservative. With all the possible varieties of stocks and bonds, it can be challenging to build a diversified portfolio by buying individual stocks and bonds when you are starting with small amounts of money to invest. Fortunately, the investment industry has created the following helpful tools to make it easier.

Mutual Fund Investing

Mutual funds are securities that can make it easier for an individual investor to build a diversified portfolio. A mutual fund is a security created by an investment company to buy a large number of securities, usually stocks or bonds, with a specific objective. Many mutual fund shares can be purchased initially for as little as $3,000.[70] This allows investors to broadly diversify a portfolio and access professional investment managers despite having only a small amount of money to invest.

Here is one important aspect of mutual fund investing that many people miss: the term 'mutual fund' by itself does not tell you

---

[69] If a company cannot borrow money from the bank at a cheap rate, they are forced to pay a higher interest rate by selling higher-interest rate bonds to access the money they need to operate its business. There may be good reasons a bank won't lend them their money at a lower interest rate.

[70] Some funds have very high minimums, but others have initial minimum purchases at $1,000 or below.

what type of securities you are actually owning. Many times, I have heard, "I tried buying a mutual fund years ago, and it didn't work out that well, so I don't like them."

Here's the problem with that statement: A mutual fund can have a goal of buying really safe bonds, really aggressive stocks, a combination of these, or anything in between. So, you can buy a bond mutual fund or a stock mutual fund. The fund can concentrate on particular industries or invest in a broad range of companies. Without knowing the type of mutual fund you own, you cannot honestly evaluate the performance.

This is both good news and bad news. There are thousands of mutual funds to choose from in the US. It may require some research, but you *can* build a good long-term portfolio with mutual funds that don't pay commissions to salespeople.[71] Find a financial planner to give you professional advice if needed.

Exchange Traded Funds

Another type of security that has recently grown significantly in popularity among investors is the Exchange Traded Fund ("ETF"). These ETFs are very similar to mutual funds in that they have a stated objective, typically buy a diversified mix of stocks or bonds, and hire professional managers. The difference from mutual funds is based on the mechanism for buying and selling, but their overall aim is the same. ETFs can provide very low-cost access to broadly diversified investments.

In 2023, you won't find ETFs inside 401k accounts, but you may be able to use them to build a good, diversified investment portfolio in an IRA or non-retirement account.

There is a lot to know about investing, but understanding these terms can help you begin to build a portfolio confidently. You aren't applying for a job as a financial advisor, though, so let's

---

[71] These are called no-load mutual funds.

talk about what you should *do now* to start building your portfolio.

Investing in Action

Once you have margin set aside and have identified the amount of risk you want to take and the types of accounts you should use, you still have to invest. Jump off the log! You don't want to just decide to invest, you want to do it. Let's take time to discuss how you should approach investing, how to structure your investments, and how to allocate your investments.

Three Ways You Must Approach Investing

As you start investing, you want to make sure you invest early (that means now), invest regularly, and invest aggressively.

Invest Early (that means now)

The power of compounding is amazing. Albert Einstein reportedly said, "Compound interest is the eighth wonder of the world. He who understands it earns it . . . he who doesn't . . . pays it." To take advantage of compounding interest you need capital and time. You provide the capital by creating margin. You maximize the time by starting early.

An illustration of the power of compounding should convince you.[72] If on January 1, when you are 25 years old, you contribute $4,000 to an investment account that earns 8% annually and continue to add $4,000 annually on the first of the year, you will have contributed $164,000 to the account by the time you turn 66. Your investment account balance at age 66 will be over $1,200,000.

As amazing as this ending balance is, the commitment to begin investing at age twenty-five is pivotal to that end result. If this same investor delayed starting the annual investments from age 25 to age 30 - just waiting five years reduces the total invested

---

[72] Details of this illustration are in Appendix 2.

by $20,000 - the ending balance at age 66 would drop from $1,200,000 to just over $800,000.[73]

There is no substitute for starting early and the earlier you start, the more dramatic the results. At age 45, starting to invest $4,000 annually allows you to accumulate a balance of just over $217,000 at age 66. Not bad. But that 45-year-old will need a lot more money to invest to achieve the same future investment balance of $1,200,000 that the 25-year-old enjoyed.

The advantage of starting young is having an extra five to ten (or even twenty) more years to invest. The cost of waiting to invest isn't that you have $20,000 less to spend in your late twenties - it's that you have $400,000 less at age 65.

In the end, you don't miss out on the first ten years of growth, you miss out on the last ten years of growth. In other words, missing out on an 8% return on a $4,000 or $8,000 balance seems tolerable. It is the 8% return you don't get on an $800,000 portfolio when you are in your sixties that is really costly.

> In the end, you don't miss out on the first ten years of growth…It is the 8% return you don't get on the $800,000 portfolio when you are 60 years old.

The encouragement to start investing early and aggressively is not an invitation to accumulate wealth for wealth's sake. Your investments should be targeted toward God-given goals; these investments can provide you with the freedom

---

[73] And, by the way, if a 22-year-old starts investing $4,000 a year until age 66 as illustrated above, the extra $12,000 of contributions made at ages 22, 23, and 24, drive the ending balance at age 66 up to $1,542,042.

necessary. The less you accumulate in investments, the less financial flexibility you will have later in life.

Invest Regularly

Make it a habit. If you have conviction goals - or just goals with margin - set up automatic transfers. Doing this allows you to make a singular, one-time decision to add $200 a month into a college savings account as a conviction goal, rather than twelve monthly decisions about how much you *feel* can be transferred.

> ...your goals dictate your spending, not the other way around.

You are more likely to build that college fund by contributing $200 monthly if you set up the transfers on auto-draft. Just make it a '1-mile-a-day' goal. Set up the monthly $200 transfer from your checking account into your education account and move on. The alternative is to spend money on everything you can come up with, and then, if there is some extra leftover, add it to your savings. Now that's looking like a 'Tortilla Chip' goal, isn't it? Don't just decide you want to invest $200 a month in your college fund, jump off the log and actually invest it.

Monthly transfers can apply to a savings goal or an investment goal that adds to a retirement account or an education account, builds a non-retirement account, or adds extra principal on a loan payment. Make the commitment to direct your income to these places when you are sitting at the kitchen table looking at your goals and your budget - not when you are looking up your checking account balance on the 27th of the month counting the days until your next paycheck. Setting up automatic transfers helps reinforce that your goals dictate your spending, not the other way around.

I have met many in their twenties who are interested in accumulating wealth but not very interested in investing regularly. This is how it has played out: They made a one-time investment of about $1,500 in a high-flying technology mutual fund (or bought some crypto) several years ago. Years have gone by, but since the wealth has not materialized from the initial $1,500 investment, they begin to sour on investing. They had a romanticized notion that they could buy a magical investment and make it grow. An initial investment is important, of course, but you have to regularly add to your investments to accumulate assets for far-off goals; one-time or sporadic investments do not have the same long-term effect.

Invest Aggressively

By having goals and creating margin at a young age, your most valuable asset, perhaps, is time. Take advantage of this by building an aggressive portfolio. Don't overthink it. As your goals crystalize and your savings and investment balances grow, you can cater your strategy to your specific goals at a given time - but begin and stay aggressive as you invest for long-term goals.

Of course, you need to match your portfolio risk with your goals and time horizon, and you need to create a diversified portfolio, but you want to be as aggressive with your investments as you can stomach while you are young.

Building appropriate savings balances and creating regular margin allows you to invest more aggressively and do it responsibly.

How Should you Structure your Savings and Investments?

Think of structuring your savings and investments using three buckets. When looking at these buckets from above, place your emergency and major purchase savings in the leftmost bucket. In the center bucket, place your non-retirement investments - some may be general in nature, and some may be specific. In the rightmost bucket, place your retirement investments.

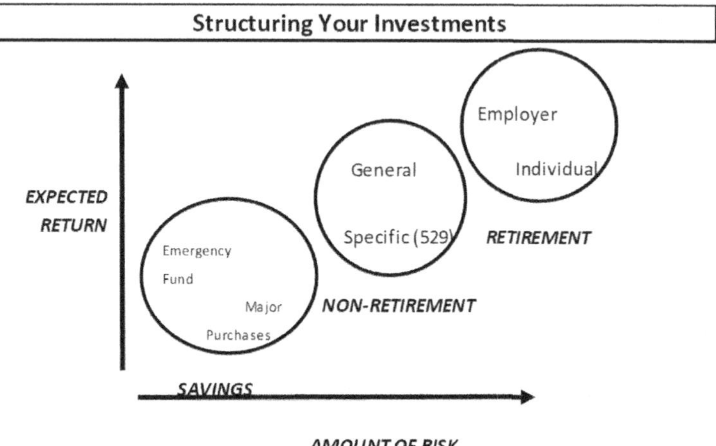

By arranging these buckets in a diagonal fashion, you can see the desired risk and return characteristics of each bucket. The labels and locations of these buckets provide a visual reminder of how aggressively you want to invest each account.

Clearly, on the conservative side, your savings portion on the lower left is not really invested. Rather, it is getting the best return available for a no-risk deposit account. In the middle, you are seeking a decent return and you are willing to assume some risk. Your long-term retirement investments belong in the bucket that assumes more risk but provides a higher expected return.

Some investors are tempted to skip the two leftmost buckets and get right to the more exciting investment opportunities where higher returns, over time, are more realistic. This can be dangerous for many reasons.

Skipping the emergency fund increases the likelihood that the investor will have to invade the long-term investment bucket to pay for an unexpected expense. This can force the investor to withdraw from a long-term, aggressive investment bucket after only a short period of time. This may force the investor to sell an aggressive investment at an inopportune time; investment returns can be very unpredictable over short periods of time. Even investments that will end up performing well (as expected) will have periods of time when they perform poorly, since this is just part of the ebbs and flows of the market's normal movements.

Building an appropriate emergency fund allows you to give your aggressive investment enough time to provide the desired return. As a result, the presence of an emergency fund is a major contributor to allowing you to persevere and eventually enjoy the returns that should come from prudent, long-term investing.

Descriptions of Populated Portfolios

Short of becoming a professional financial analyst, how can you populate a portfolio that can provide the expected returns you desire with an acceptable amount of risk? You want the best return you can get, and you want peace of mind with your investments. You also have limits, and you may rather devote time to your other responsibilities and endeavors than researching, analyzing, monitoring, and implementing your investment portfolio. As your portfolio balances grow and the stakes are higher, seeking professional advice from a competent financial planner may make sense.[74]

Hiring a competent professional advisor may be unrealistic as you start out. Let's explore a few starting places for you to consider as you build your own portfolio.

Savings - As discussed previously, FDIC-insured, high-yield savings accounts are attractive for this. Buying CDs may provide a slightly higher return, but they also add an element of risk because they come with certain holding period limitations.[75]

---

[74] If you are curious, the six steps to fix a broken record courtesy of an internet search are: 1. Stabilize. 2. Apply epoxy. 3. Smooth epoxy. 4. Let the epoxy dry. 5. Play the record. 6. Remove excess epoxy.

[75] Most financial emergencies are unscheduled. This contributes to the 'emergency' part of a financial emergency. And 'time deposits' like CDs or certain I-Bonds limit your access to your money.

Long-Term Retirement - While savings is the most conservative bucket on the risk vs. return chart, long-term retirement is the most aggressive investment category because it has the longest time horizon. Picking specific investments in your employer-provided retirement plan requires you to select funds from the limited menu of funds. Research the available funds and select ones that provide broad exposure to US and Foreign stock markets. Index funds are acceptable. Generally, you want to invest in funds that provide exposure to the overall markets - not just a smaller section.

For retirement accounts like IRAs and Roth IRAs, invest with an aggressive approach. Instead of investing in concentrated positions, invest in a collection of aggressive US and Foreign stock mutual funds. Mutual funds, remember, are inherently diversified since they own dozens or sometimes hundreds of stocks. Strive to include funds that give you exposure to a mix of both large and small stocks in your funds. Stock index funds can be suitable for these investments. Mixing US and Foreign stock exposure equally is not a crazy notion as the composition of the global equity markets are about 50% US and 50% Foreign.[76]

Non-retirement investing - Investing in the center of the risk vs. return chart can be the trickiest because the time frames can vary significantly based on your goals or circumstances. For goals with a 10+ year time horizon, invest with US and Foreign stock mutual funds or ETFs like in a retirement portfolio. For goals with a time horizon shorter than ten years, mix in bond funds to temper your overall risk. The table below may provide a reasonable outline to select diversified funds. You may choose to split the stock target percentage between US and Foreign Stock funds.

---

[76] Professional portfolios may include exposures to other asset classes to further diversify the portfolio. These often include investments in commodities and real estate funds among others. When your portfolio grows to be $30,000 or more, this type of additional diversification makes more sense.

Expected Time Horizon	Target Bond %	Target Stock %
10+ Years	0%	100%
6-9 Years	20%	80%
3-5 Years	50%	50%
1-3 Years	75%	25%

In non-retirement accounts, identify low-cost mutual funds or ETFs that provide broad exposure to the desired investment. Every transaction in a non-retirement account may create tax consequences, so be careful how often you buy and sell securities in these accounts.

In 529 education accounts, you will pick from a menu as well. 529 accounts often allow you to invest in an 'age-weighted' strategy which starts with an aggressive portfolio when the child beneficiary is young. The strategy will automatically shift the portfolio to a more conservative mix as the child gets closer to the expected use of the assets around age 18. These age-weighted strategies can be appealing. You don't want to lose track of the risk level and inadvertently have a 100% stock mix for a seventeen-year-old one year before using these funds for tuition.

Once you have a plan in place - including '1-mile-a-day' automatic transfers into these accounts - schedule a time every three to six months to review your portfolios. In these reviews, research the performance of your securities and compare their returns to returns of comparable funds or a relevant index. Calculate how far your portfolio has drifted from the desired target allocation and adjust as necessary.

Investing Wrap-Up

If you think the choices for a drink at a local coffee shop are complex, you may be overwhelmed by the number of possible securities to buy in your portfolio. Implementing an investment portfolio can seem overwhelming, but the long-term results make it worth the effort.

Reminder of Goals

Just as your investment goals drive how much you invest (see Chapter 3), these goals should drive how you build your investment portfolios and what securities you buy. With appropriate savings balances for emergencies and upcoming major purchases, you can invest for retirement, education, and other long-term goals with confidence.

The longer-term the goals, the more risk you can accept as you build your portfolio. If done sensibly, this should provide higher investment returns *over the long term.*

Micah Williams ran 100 meters in an amazing 10.11 seconds at the 2021 NCAA Outdoor Track and Field Championship. He was awarded third place.

Cole Hocker became a national champion at that same meet by running the 1500-meter race in a time of 3:35.35 to win first place. No one ever runs a 1500-meter race by running the exact same time for each of the fifteen 100-meter sections of the race; but if Cole Hocker had done this on his way to victory, he would have run fifteen consecutive 100-meter dashes each in a time of 14.35 seconds. So, the national champion of the 1500-meter race was over 3 seconds slower in the 100 meters than the third-place finisher in the 100-meter race![77]

[77] And when they are running that fast, three seconds is a long distance. That's about 20% of the length of the straightaway.

If Micah had run his 100-meter race while Cole was running down the straight away as a part of his four lap 1500-meter race, it would have appeared that Micah was running extremely fast, and that Cole was running very slowly. You would not have predicted that the faster runner would end up 3rd place and that the slower runner would be the National Champion.

In order to evaluate how fast each runner was actually running, we need to know how far each runner was setting out to run. Which runner was faster? The answer may be different if we were evaluating each runner over 1500 meters instead of 100 meters. It is easy to make the same mistake when evaluating investments. You need to evaluate each investment account and investment security in the context of your goals and time horizon.

Many of your long-term investments will have time periods in which they don't go up or down much. There will even be time periods when these investments drop significantly. We would be very alarmed if a long-distance runner actually reversed course during a race, but it is normal for good, prudent investments to perform in this way for some periods of time. If you are investing for the long-term, you want a marathon runner - even if it appears she is running *relatively* slowly at certain times.

Similarly, conservative and moderately aggressive investments should be evaluated differently from aggressive, long-term investments. As tempting as it may be to compare these against the performance of the high-flying stock of the day, evaluate your short and mid-term investments with reasonable expectations. These investments will not grow as much as more aggressive investments when markets are rising.

Finally, don't evaluate a bond fund or a high-yield savings account against the returns of the stock market. You can easily draw wrong conclusions about the quality and suitability of these investments - just like you might make the same mistake at a track meet.

Exhortation Five

PLAN YOUR ESTATE

Two different college classes are graded like this:

> Course One - 100% of the semester grade is based on an exam given on the last day of class covering only the last five lectures.
>
> Course Two - The semester grade for the class is broken down into three components:
>
> > ⅓ for participation in the first fifteen classes
> >
> > ⅓ for a group project due after class thirty
> >
> > ⅓ for a comprehensive final exam taken during the last class

Most people think estate planning is done by old, rich people. You would be shocked to learn how many responsible, productive adults who take their stewardship responsibilities seriously have not prepared any formal estate planning documents. Surprisingly, many who *have* thoughtfully prepared legal documents have failed to tell loved ones where to find these documents or how to access them. Even those without any estate planning documents prepared have an estate plan. In short, it states, "I will let other people decide how and when my estate assets will be distributed and who will raise my children if I have any." Your kind and benevolent state government has laws in place to distribute your assets (and your children) if you do not leave behind properly executed estate documents. Considering that your final estate distribution is your last, and probably the largest, financial decision during your lifetime, the default state-administered estate rules are not sufficient for a steward. The occasion deserves some planning and attention.[78]

Documents for an Estate Plan

If you are living outside of your parents' home (or should be), or have your own checking account or a car, you need to prepare certain legal documents. These include a will and two directives that allow others to make decisions for you if incapacitated. Each directive is called a 'power of attorney' document.[79]

If your situation is very simple, you might consider writing your own documents or using an online service to help you create the documents you want. If you create your own documents, you must take steps to execute the documents properly in your state. My suggestion is that you talk to an attorney in your home state about preparing the documents for you. As a twenty-something, the content of the documents is probably very simple, and the decisions necessary to complete them are fairly easy.

---

[78] If you have minor children, or other dependents, naming guardians to care for them is your top priority and biggest stewardship decision. Do not leave it to the court to decide who will raise your children. (Can you imagine two sets of in-laws arguing for custody of a small child before a judge!?!?)

[79] One for healthcare and one for financial decision-making. The plural is 'powers-of-attorney' documents.

Legacy to Others is more than Money

Adults with children or grandchildren leave behind three things to the successive generations: financial capital, social capital, and spiritual capital.[80]

In short, financial capital consists of your assets (and sometimes liabilities). The most common assets left to others include cash, non-retirement investments, life insurance proceeds, a home (or equity in a home), and/or retirement assets like a 401(k) or IRA. Financial capital is the most common aspect people associate with estate planning, and it is most often passed on to family members or charities at death.[81]

Social capital is the ability to relate to others. This certainly includes the ability to communicate well and relate well with family, friends, elders, professional co-workers, superiors, subordinates, authorities, etc. The ability to work well, and even thrive, in relationships is a very important skill most commonly (and easily) taught by parents and family to children. Teaching personal skills can be challenging. It is easiest to do when a child is very young.

Spiritual capital is a proper understanding of, and ability to relate to, your Creator and faith community. Developing spiritual capital also includes interaction with the faith community. As a Christian, this means knowing God and understanding what a grace-filled relationship with God looks like. Further, this means relating to and integrating with a faith community that involves sacrifice, transparency, and service among other things. This can be messy at times because life is messy, and people are messy. Knowledge, traditions, and spiritual disciplines are best

---

[80] This is wonderfully addressed in Russ Crosson's *A Life Well Spent*.

[81] In the case of a married couple, the first death usually leaves all assets to the surviving spouse. At the second death, assets are usually left to family members, and possibly charities.

communicated and modeled to children while they are young, but spiritual capital can be developed at any age.

Ranking the Legacy and the Timing

From a parent's perspective, financial, social, and spiritual capital are not all equally important. While people may not agree on the relative importance of these three, everyone would have particular reasons for the order in which they rank them. I am convinced that financial capital is the least important of the three things you leave behind.

If an adult child lacks appropriate social and spiritual capital, acquiring sizable financial capital always creates significant problems. If a child has appropriate social and spiritual capital, she can more easily handle significant financial capital, but she can also handle receiving little or no financial capital.

If an adult child lacks appropriate social and spiritual capital, acquiring sizable financial capital always creates problems.

Timing makes estate planning difficult. While most people don't think they need to plan their estates until they are old and have lots of assets, *they are leaving their children the two most important things when they are young and most likely broke*. Parents try to love their children from birth and cultivate in their children social and spiritual capital even if they don't associate these traits with estate planning. The social and spiritual capital that is 'taught' and hopefully 'caught' lays the groundwork for the successful transfer of the financial capital in later years.

A parent may consider their estate planning messy when their adult child is struggling in various ways. Perhaps the child:

- does not earn enough to live outside the home.
- struggles with basic life skills like paying a bill on time or getting an oil change for the car.
- is unable to have conversations about serious life issues and prefers to withdraw.
- changes jobs every six months.
- struggles to communicate with neighbors, co-workers, or a boss who is 15 years older.
- struggles with depression or mental health issues.
- struggles with chemical dependency or addiction.
- has had frequent arrests.

None of these examples above signal failure on the part of the parents, but these social issues affect how parents leave assets to their children. Parents do not want to leave $500,000 to a 27-year-old who struggles with chemical addictions because this financial legacy will not be a blessing to the child.

The Estate Planning Surprise

Another common estate planning challenge is what I call the 'estate planning surprise'. Picture a 55-year-old couple living in a $350,000 house (fully paid for) with $50,000 in savings. Additionally, this 55-year-old couple has life insurance that pays a death benefit of $500,000, and their combined retirement accounts total $600,000. While this couple has only $50,000 of assets available for their own use, they actually have an estate net worth of $1,500,000.

This couple has done a great job eliminating all debt and saving well for retirement, but in 2023 suburban America this couple does not appear to others (or to themselves) to be very wealthy. The home equity, life insurance proceeds, and retirement accounts are not available to them right now. They can only access and spend the $50,000 in the checking account.

If this couple has two twentysomething children at the time they pass away, the financial capital that passes to their children would provide $750,000 to each child. This surprises many couples because they 'only' have $50,000 in available wealth. Without advance planning, each child would receive $450,000 of immediate cash (savings, home equity, and life insurance proceeds) and $300,000 of retirement money.

The parents' discipline of paying down the debt and living like they were not wealthy is not so easily 'passed' to the kids. The two twentysomethings start with significantly more cash and opportunity than the seasoned, experienced parents ever had. You can probably guess that the 'kids' may not make the best decisions with access to this much wealth and so little experience.[82]

The common response this is usually either, "I am sure they will use restraint and get good help," or "Yikes! That won't go very well. Can you make sure they don't do stupid things with the money?"[83]

If just one child is struggling with their independence regarding adult responsibilities or relationships, a parent's freedom to leave financial capital becomes complicated. If the maturity level of an adult child makes a parent hesitant to loan them their cell phone, car, or golf clubs, or have them house-sit for two weeks, the prospect of leaving large amounts of unrestricted money to a child should be very troubling.

Whatever spiritual capital a child exhibits, the parent should evaluate how these differences influence their desire to provide a financial blessing to their child. It is common for parents to realize that their children have not adopted and embraced their

---

[82] A favorite quote of mine attributed to Warren Buffet says, "When a man with money meets a man with experience. . . . The man with the money gets the experience, and the man with the experience gets the money."

[83] No. I cannot. The parents must address this the best they can in their estate documents.

spiritual beliefs or faith traditions. This can present itself in many ways:

- A child may embrace Christianity with greater zeal than their parents.
- A child may walk away from the church.
- A child may profess alignment with an entirely different religion.

In most cases, a perceived deficiency in spiritual capital is less problematic than deficiencies in social capital because inheriting money won't necessarily put the child in physical danger. All parents have to evaluate this for themselves.

What Does all this Mean?

The most important aspect of estate planning at a young age is equipping your children with social and spiritual capital. If this good foundation is laid, the task of leaving financial assets to children that will serve as a blessing to them will be exponentially easier. If the social and spiritual capital are not grasped well by children, you may find yourself twisting and contorting clauses in expansive (and expensive) trust documents to limit your children's access to large amounts of assets at a young age.

Drafting estate documents can be straightforward or quickly become a real challenge.[84] Drafting them to accommodate more complex family dynamics is almost impossible. Get your estate documents prepared, but don't think these documents contain the entire estate plan. You also leave more important things that can't be written down by an attorney.

---

[84] That's why hiring an attorney to assist is so important.

Course One - 100% of the semester grade is based on an exam given on the last day of class covering only the last five lectures.

A college class with 100% of the semester grade based on one final exam. Sound awful? Cruel and unusual? Barbaric? Seems like the intense pressure of that final exam would make the most prepared and disciplined academic wilt under pressure.

A typical college student would wait until the end of the class to get serious about preparing for the final exam. Many people approach their estate planning the same way. "When I'm old and rich, I'll call in an expensive attorney and she can sort it all out for us - just like in the movies."

In reality, older rich people often end up having to contort legal documents to protect their children from their money because their children aren't exhibiting good social and spiritual capital.

If your final exam score dictates your grade for the class, you need everything to go right on that exam. It is possible to enter the final exam with no possibility of getting the final grade you want. And so it is with your estate planning. If the social and spiritual capital developed in an adult child are disappointing, the final asset distribution may not meet your expectations.

The way to earn a passing grade with estate planning is to realize that the progress along the way dictates the real significance of the final exam. Similar to the grading for Course Two - earning good marks on the first two components of the final grade for the class makes the final exam less stressful.

A broad view of estate planning reveals that the most important legacy most people leave loved ones has nothing to do with money, and it is often left forty years before financial assets are distributed. *The most important part of what a person leaves behind at death is non-financial* and it is generally left so early that no one is thinking of vast sums of assets.[85]

[85] I know. Most parents work very hard at raising their children to be good people - social and spiritual capital and the like. They just rarely think of this as part of their estate planning. Without turning parenting into a mechanical process designed to create vessels to dump money into at our death (sounds awful!), recognize that loving, nurturing, and training your children is a huge contribution to the legacy you leave behind. This should heighten the sense of significance to family and child raising.

Conclusion

WRAPPING UP

Money is important. Consistently heeding the five easy-to-understand exhortations will make a significant difference in your financial life.

1. Give charitably.
2. Set and take action on financial goals.
3. Create margin.
4. Save and invest your margin.
5. Plan your estate.

Money is important. There are many things, however, that are more important.

Your goals are more important than money. The values that dictate your most important financial goals compel you to use your money in particular ways. Chapters 2, 3, and 4 exhort you to identify the values that you cherish most ***and*** to act on them. Begin making decisions today that will create the long-term outcomes you most desire. Jump off the log!

Other people are more important than money. Charitable giving and proper estate planning discussed in Chapters 1 and 5 recognize the immense value of other people. The impact of your charitable giving – tax deductible or not – blesses other people. Cultivating a broader view of estate planning recognizes that you leave behind so much more than money.

You are more important than money. Your financial decisions impact your life and your relationships. Using money responsibly and using it in a manner consistent with your goals is uniquely personal.

Chapter 1 exhorts you to give charitably. Sacrificial giving blesses other people, but it also provides a blessing to you. The God of the Bible is not needy. God is not lacking anything. The Bible does not command and encourage you to give because God needs the money. God is more interested in your mind, your heart, and your soul than He is interested in your financial transactions. The Bible teaches that the practice of generosity will help you become more unselfish and more Christlike.

My desire is that you can identify ***your*** most important financial goals and that you can use your resources to express what you truly value and find important.

Appendix One

TIPS ON TACKLING PERIODIC EXPENSES

Spending categories that contain periodic expenses very commonly act as 'budget killers'. There are two different kinds of periodic expenses:

- Scheduled periodic expenses are specific expenses you plan to incur at a particular time. Common scheduled periodic expenses include Christmas, travel and vacation, gifts for birthdays or anniversaries, certain car and home expenses, as well as some insurance and taxes.
- Unscheduled periodic expenses occur at unknown times and often in unknown amounts. The most common unscheduled periodic expenses include repairs and maintenance related to your car and home.

Scheduled periodic expenses, even when anticipated, are challenging because discipline is required to prepare for them. If your budget has $600 allocated for Christmas, you can't wait until November to set the cash aside for these purchases. You won't have room in your November and December cash flow to pull out $300 each month to pay for these expenses.

Preparing for these scheduled periodic expenses can be addressed with some planning and discipline. You can prepare $600 for holiday spending by including $50 a month in your spending budget. This is the easy part. The challenge is making sure you don't spend that $50 of Christmas money in your January budget on something else.

It is more difficult to prepare for unscheduled periodic expenses. How do you prepare for car repairs when the timing of any repairs and the amounts are unknown? Your old car may chug along for two more years, or it may die tomorrow. The older your car, the more you need to prepare your budget for some car repairs.

Preparing for Periodic Expenses

If you prepare for the annual $600 spending for Christmas by allocating $50 of cash flow for Christmas each month during the year, your November 1st checking account balance will include $500 dollars that are committed to Christmas spending. Again, this is simple enough to understand, but it is difficult to implement for two reasons. People often make spending decisions by looking at their checking account balance. "Hey, we have a huge checking account balance, let's take a quick getaway next weekend and drive on the Blue Ridge Parkway. We can stay in a bed and breakfast." Usually, people have multiple periodic expenses that are simultaneously accumulating unspent dollars each month and spending accumulated dollars each month. This quickly makes the tracking complex.

There are ways to remedy these two difficulties, but they do take some effort. The effort (and the math) involved isn't as hard as organic chemistry; you really just need to understand two things.

Tracking your spending and checking your account balance are two different things. Do not attempt to answer the question, "Can we afford to pay for . . .?" based on the current balance in your checking account. Track your spending, and regularly compare your actual spending against the budgeted spending targets. Whether you use formal budget software tools or apps to track all your spending or do it manually, monitor your progress. Proper planning for periodic expenses will inflate your checking account balance in months when you don't spend any money. This is likely to happen in February if you plan on $50 a month for a $600 Christmas budget.

Relying on mentally tracking your progress towards periodic expenses is doomed to failure. You may think, "I like Christmas so much, I will keep track of the money set aside for Christmas so I will be prepared. I won't confuse these savings with anything else because I love Christmas!" Even with your mental acumen and your killer math skills, this will not work. You will probably end up with at least five to ten periodic expense categories that will all have a monthly budget allocation. In some months you will spend money in some of these categories, but in others, you will not spend any money allowing your cash balances will continue to build up.

You are now thinking, "Is there a good way to stay on top of these periodic expenses? How can someone prepare for these?" You can prepare by doing two things: track all of the money budgeted and spent in each periodic category, and physically move budgeted periodic expense money out of your checking account on a regular basis.

Preparing for scheduled periodic expenses is easy to understand. Using our Christmas example, you have $50 set aside for Christmas in January, but you don't spend any of it. Therefore, you physically transfer $50 from your checking account (as if it has been spent) to a separate savings account that you nickname "Christmas." You continue to transfer $50 each month from your checking account to your savings account nicknamed "Christmas". At the end of April, you will have $200 in your Christmas account.

As you spend money for Christmas, you would simply transfer money out of your Christmas savings account to pay for the expenses. If you use a credit card for your purchases, transfer money from your designated Christmas savings account to the checking account that you use to pay your credit card bill.

Preparing for unscheduled periodic expenses is harder. You may budget $100 a month for car maintenance because you want to be prepared for $1,200 in car repairs for the year. Your car may break down at inconvenient times, however, like when you have only $200 set aside after two months. Timing is not the only uncertainty with unscheduled periodic expenses. The repair may actually cost $1,500 instead of the budgeted $1,200. In addition to a good budget that accounts for appropriate categories, an appropriate emergency fund balance provides help in these situations.

Specific Steps to Prepare

The number of savings accounts you use for these periodic expenses is up to you. Some people like having eight distinct savings accounts (with eight distinct nicknames) because these can provide so much clarity. Others like the simplicity of using only one savings account that they supplement with a monthly accounting that breaks down the contents of the one account balance. For example, instead of four accounts:

1. $200 Christmas
2. $350 Vacation
3. $250 Car Repair
4. $ 50 Home Repair Items

They maintain one account with a balance of $850 and scribble down the details for the four category balances each month. Since each of these four categories should have money added each month and one or more of the categories may have money withdrawn for actual expenses each month, the monthly reconciliation can get a bit complicated. Because I love simplicity, I prefer one account for each periodic expense. It is easy to locate competitive online savings accounts that allow you to open multiple accounts[86] and name each to suit your needs.

As you understand the mechanics of identifying which budget categories are periodic and how to keep track of the money allocated to each category, you may see why I call these designated savings accounts 'Build-Up' accounts. In a perfect world, you allow these balances to build up to the desired balance, then you use the accumulated balance to pay cash for the expenses. To answer, "When can we afford to spend $1,000 on a vacation? When can we use $7,000 to buy a car? When can we . . . ?" you simply look at the balance in the appropriate 'Build-Up' account.

Despite the imperfections of the system, the use of 'Build-Up' accounts can help you physically set aside budget amounts for important budget categories, provide clarity, and help you be prepared for the expenses when they occur. Ultimately, the 'Build-Up' accounts are a tool to help compensate for the timing differences between when you earn your money and when these periodic expenses actually occur.

---

[86] This may be a savings account at a local bank or high-yield savings account popular among online banks. Look for FDIC-insured accounts with the highest rates. You can often set up automatic monthly transfers in advance to simplify your work.

Appendix Two

COMPOUND INTEREST ILLUSTRATED

If you invested $4,000 on the first day of the year as a 25-year-old and continued adding $4,000 every January 1 through age 66, you would accumulate an investment account worth $1,212,990 if you earned 8% every year.[87] This disregards any fees and all taxes. (See Table A2.1 on the next page.)

Total contributions of $164,000 grow to $1,212,990 by age 66 with an 8% annual return. Granted, it is usually easier to save $4,000 annually as a 60-year-old than a 25-year-old, but the long-term effect of compounding interest is amazing.

---

[87] Some rows in the table A2.1 are not shown for spacing purposes. The rows in italics show where certain years are not shown. The compounding at 8% excludes any consideration for fees and taxes that you may encounter when investing - so the 8% annual return would be after all fees and taxes.

Table A2.1

Investing $4,000 on First Day of Year				
Age	Beginning	Contribution	Gain @ 8%	Ending
25	-	4,000	320	4,320
26	4,320	4,000	666	8,986
27	8,986	4,000	1,039	14,025
28	14,025	4,000	1,442	19,467
29	19,467	4,000	1,877	25,344
30	25,344	4,000	2,348	31,692
40	117,300	4,000	9,704	131,004
50	315,822	4,000	25,586	345,408
60	744,419	4,000	59,874	808,293
65	1,119,139	4,000	89,851	**1,212,990**
		164,000		

To illustrate that compounding interest has such a dramatic effect over a long period of time, consider investing $6,000 each year instead of $4,000. A balance of over $1.2 million sounds pretty good with 'only' regular, consistent $4,000 annual investments. Increasing the annual investment from $4,000 to $6,000 has a similarly impressive result with an annual return of 8% in Table A2.2 on the following page.

Notice that when you increase the annual contribution by 50% (increasing from $4,000 to $6,000 is a 50% increase), the ending balance also goes up by the same 50% from $1.2 million to $1.8 million.

The math is not just interesting, it is motivational. After all, what if you invested the same $4,000 every single year and you invested in the exact same investment, but you just waited until later to start? How bad could that be? Notice that this would eventually require you to make the same cash flow sacrifices and expose yourself to the same level of investment risk.

Table A2.2

Investing $6,000 on First Day of Year				
Age	Beginning	Contribution	Gain @ 8%	Ending
25	-	6,000	480	6,480
26	6,480	6,000	998	13,478
27	13,478	6,000	1,558	21,036
28	21,036	6,000	2,163	29,199
29	29,199	6,000	2,816	38,015
30	38,015	6,000	3,521	47,536
40	175,946	6,000	14,556	196,502
50	473,727	6,000	38,378	518,105
60	1,116,614	6,000	89,809	1,212,423
65	1,678,688	6,000	134,775	**1,819,463**
		246,000		

If you invested in the same way as in the first example but you delayed the first $4,000 contribution until you were 30 years old instead of 25, your balance at age 65 is quite a bit lower. In Table A2.3 the rightmost column shows the results when starting at age 30 instead of 25:

Table A2.3

Investing $4,000 on First Day of Year - ***But Wait 5 Years***				
Age	Beginning	Contribution	Gain @ 8%	Ending
25		*0*		*0*
26		*0*		*0*
27		*0*		*0*
28		*0*		*0*
29		*0*		*0*
30		4,000	320	4,320
40	62,583	4,000	5,327	71,910
50	197,695	4,000	16,136	217,831
60	489,391	4,000	39,471	532,862
65	744,419	4,000	59,874	**808,293**
		144,000		

So, instead of investing $164,000 to achieve an age-66 balance of $1,212,990, you invest $20,000 less but achieve a balance of $808,293. In a sense, failing to invest the $4,000 over those five years gave you $20,000 for consumption in your late twenties, but it cost you over $404,000 of assets at age 66.

Waiting to invest can be more costly than you realize!

In real life, missing opportunities to invest at a young age can create additional challenges down the road. It is common to meet people in their thirties, forties, and fifties who feel pressured to invest very aggressively in order to "make up for lost time." The sensation of being behind on important long-term goals (and the actual reality of it) can compel an investor to speculate or simply take on more risk than their God-given temperament should bear. This out-sized investment risk can be harmful if, and when, the markets suffer cyclical declines.[88]

[88] In my adult life, we have seen massive stock market declines surrounding the dot-com bubble, the Great Financial Crisis and COVID-19. Future markets will also experience significant declines as part of natural free-market investment cycles.

ACKNOWLEDGEMENTS

Thanks to "BMoney" - What good is the right stewardship perspective if it is not communicated effectively? Thanks for the invaluable perspective and (just enough) encouragement to help me complete this '1-Mile-a-Day' goal.

Thanks to Mark and Richard - My stewardship journey did not start until my faith journey began. Thanks for your pursuit of and investment in me.

Thanks to Kenny - You are a great friend and perpetual sounding board. Even though we almost always think alike, your perspective is a catalyst for good thinking and communication.

Thanks to Dave, Tom, and Derek - Your friendship, guidance, and encouragement to pursue Christ is an inspiration.

Thanks to Boppy – You are a great model of discipline – one mile at a time. Thanks to Mo – Your gentle spirit and perceptive counsel make me jealous. Thanks to Mimi and Grammy – You are always tireless in your service to others.

Thanks to Carlton, Bradley, and Susan. Our daily work is fun but challenging. It is a joy to labor with you and wrestle with important life-altering matters every day.

Special thanks to Debbie, Hannah and Sam, Leah and Mitchell, and Elizabeth. My personal interest and vocational pursuit of understanding stewardship is not solely my own. God works in families to care for us and transform us. You are a gift to me, and I love the way you help me grow. Thanks for tolerating all that I am!

ABOUT THE AUTHOR

William B. Ertel

In 2002, Will founded Tassel Capital Management to serve middle-market and affluent individuals and families by providing financial planning and investment management assistance.

Will obtained his CPA license in 1995, his CERTIFIED FINANCIAL PLANNER® certification in 2001, and his Certified Kingdom Advisor® designation in 2019.

Will is married to Debbie. They live in Charlotte, North Carolina where they make Christ Covenant Church (PCA) their church home. Will's three daughters are actively involved in churches where they live - currently on a Naval base in California, a camp and conference center near Brevard, North Carolina, and a college campus on Lookout Mountain, Georgia.

The desire to write *Resolve* was borne out of a desire to help Will's three daughters and their spouses think Biblically about financial stewardship.